Paprika!

Essential Hungarian Flavors
Cookbook

Recipes by Members of
**The First Hungarian Reformed Church
of Cleveland**

Text by Julianna Kovach Zingale   Culinary Assistance by Mark Shary

To Him,
for His glorious mercy,
eternal love and His blessings
for our endurance inspired by hope
in our Lord Jesus Christ.

Acknowledgments

First Printing November, 2010

ISBN 978-0-615-41067-8

Published by the First Hungarian Reformed Church of Cleveland

Printed in the United States of America

For additional copies of this book, contact:

The First Hungarian Reformed Church
14530 Alexander Road
Walton Hills, OH 44146-4921
440.786.7272

paprikacookbook@att.net

Four generations of members of the First Hungarian Reformed Church of Cleveland provided the recipes contained in this book; their names follow each recipe. Additionally, we graciously thank those who contributed time, effort and support:

The Church Aid Society/ Templom Szégelyző, which includes the noodle makers; the Lorántffy Zsuzsanna Society; the Women's Guild; the Doughnut Makers;

Elaine Galgany, Elisabeth Biro, Ethel Nagy and Violet Sarosi for verifying Hungarian recipe titles;

Laura Vadaj, for her eloquent editing and precise proofreading expertise;

Betty Rose Galgany and the late Bill Koteles, who shared exquisite out-of-print cookbooks, video and samples of Hungarian embroidery designs;

Jerry Takacs, whose determination and Hungarian spirit kept this cookbook alive;

the late Jim Whitney, Whitney Stained Glass, for the medallion designs for our church's stained glass, used here as ornament; and

Jim McWilliams, designer and epicurean who provided encouragement throughout this project.

Our deepest gratitude is owed to our families. They loved us, cooked for us, preserved our heritage and, most important, brought us up in the nurture and admonition of the Lord.

Contents

PAPRIKA, *the essential Hungarian spice, is synonymous with the zest, warmth and color of Hungarian cooking and culture.*

WHILE PAPRIKA IS NOT THE ONLY SEASONING USED IN HUNGARIAN COOKING, IT IS THE ONE THAT INTRODUCED THE CUISINE TO THE WORLD. FROM DELICATE TO SPICY-HOT, PAPRIKA'S BRIGHT, DEEP-RED WARMTH AND SWEETNESS ENLIVENS POPULAR DISHES SUCH AS *GULYÁS* (GOULASH), *PAPRIKÁS* (PAPRIKASH) AND STUFFED CABBAGE. HUNGARIAN PAPRIKA HAS ITS OWN HISTORY AND IS THE FINEST QUALITY PRODUCED. PAPRIKA'S UNIQUE AND IDENTIFIABLE FLAVOR AND ITS UNIVERSAL ABILITY TO COMBINE WITH A VARIETY OF INGREDIENTS AND SEASONINGS MAY ALSO EXPLAIN ITS UBIQUITOUS PRESENCE.

Influenced by centuries of history from both peasant life and the aristocratic table, Hungarian cooking began with the nomadic wandering of Asiatic Magyar tribes on the Great Hungarian Plain. Herdsmen dried provisions; stewed them in large, round kettles; and roasted meats over open fires. Hungarian cooks adopted and adapted cooking techniques and foodstuffs from invaders through centuries. The result was a cuisine of amalgamation marked by the Turkish occupation of the country, an Italian aristocratic presence during the Renaissance and French and German overtones at the time the Austro-Hungarian Empire. The infusion of flavors was recreated in innovative Hungarian style into something truly unique and then preserved by strong attachments to culture and heritage.

The Hungarian style of cooking consists of simple preparation techniques with a few ingredients that elicit deep, mellow flavors, and contrasting tastes and textures. The result is a distinguished cuisine inclusive of a variety of characteristics: rich, thick and creamy; clear and delicate; or sprightly and tart. The cookery is characterized by a diversity of soups; cooked, stuffed or seasoned vegetables; robustly seasoned meats; and slow-cooked stews with hearty sauces. Noodles or dumplings are savory or sweet; breads are full-bodied. Divinely rich pastries are filled, layered, flaky, buttery, nut-encrusted, meringue-topped, frosted or accented with confectioner's sugar.

These authentic recipes retain the flavoring traditions and style of cooking taught by Hungarian mothers and fathers through generations. Drawing on a deep love and respect for the Hungarian heritage as well as a passion for food and good eating, these recipes preserve these cultural food traditions for future generations to enjoy.

Developing Flavor Traditions

Historically, Hungary's reputation for good food began with the remarkable quality of its land, over which various factions warred for centuries. The sunny climate and the rich, fertile soil fed by the Danube and Tisza Rivers produced perfect growing conditions for exceptionally flavored fruits and vegetables. The Great Hungarian Plain, or *puszta*, provided herdsmen a green expanse to raise well-fed livestock.

During the ninth century, the nomadic Magyar tribes traveled across the continent, carrying with them dried meat and noodles, which stored indefinitely and traveled well, owing to their light weight. Herdsmen stewed their dried meat with onions and dried barley-shaped noodles called *tarhonya* in large, round-bottom kettles termed *bogrács*, which hung over an open fire. The slow stewing process brought out the flavors and reconstituted the meat and *tarhonya*. It was the origin of *gulyás* soup, which later evolved into one of Hungary's national dishes. From their eastern origins, Magyars brought with them the custom of stuffing meat into cabbage. Stewed stuffed cabbage and stuffed vegetables are still popular.

When Genghis Khan chose the Hungarian Plain as his camp headquarters during the 13th century, common Mongolian food-preparation methods, including boiling meats and raising yeast doughs, infiltrated the campfire styles. Mongolian fried dough was the precursor to the present day *lángos*. Oriental influences in food and spices, as well as design, clothing, folk music and language, remain ingrained in the Hungarian heritage and distinguish it from other Eastern European cultures.

The wedding feast at the late 15th-century marriage of the Hungarian Renaissance king, Mátyás I (Matthias), to Beatrice of Naples introduced new ingredients and a very royal style of dining. Table settings included nearly a thousand gold dishes and artisan-crafted servingware, which set the bar for formal dinners. Banquet tables were lavished with an enormous variety of highly seasoned food, livening the cuisine in a grand manner. The queen broadened the seasoning palette and expanded the flavors of Hungarian cuisine by introducing dill and garlic to court dining as well as onions, which would later become the most important vegetable in Hungarian cooking.

6

The Ottoman Turks invaded the country in the 1500s despite fierce resistance from the Hungarians. But throughout the fighting, both sides had to eat, and the Turks' long-term presence, though despised, altered cooking through the introduction of new foods and cooking techniques that Hungarians retooled to something new and different. Spitted meats and prepared pilafs were akin to the earlier Hungarian outdoor cooking methods and were easily adapted. Phyllo dough, tomatoes, corn, poppy seed, squash, rice, cherries and coffee were integrated into the cuisine as basic staples.

Enter Paprika

The Hungarian cooking repertoire continued to be transformed by cultural fusion. It was the introduction of the Turkish pepper that would forever change the nature, flavor and aroma of Hungarian cuisine.

The paprika plant had been grown ornamentally by botanists and collectors in Central Europe in the mid-1500s and later as a decoration by housewives. Paprika, the ground red pepper spice, arrived in Hungary in 1526. It was supposedly brought by the invading Turks, whose contact with the Hungarian herdsmen led to the spicing of their roasting bacon and the seasoning of the stews bubbling in their kettles. Refugees from the Balkans, fleeing the Turkish occupation of their countries, may also have brought seeds of the plant with them as they moved into Hungary. Their access to the peppers began with Columbus's transport of them from South America to Portugal and Spain through Italy to Greece. Greek seafarers may have carried the plants with them to ports. Plants growing along the Tisza and Danube Rivers allowed Hungarian fishermen to liberally season their kettles of fish stew.

The spicy-hot paprika seemingly complemented everything: beef, pork, poultry, fish and game. It provided a tantalizing aroma, color and spice. The peasants adopted it, using it in such great abundance that it totally

eclipsed the more expensive and less available black pepper and other ancient spices, including ginger, saffron and basil. Using it in its pure ground form, exclusive of other seasonings, was unique to Hungarian culture and provided a more interesting flavor than did black pepper. Paprika, with its ubiquitous presence and distinctive flavor, became Hungary's defining condiment. Hungary established Europe's

7

only chili-pepper-based cuisine. Beginning in the 17th century, Hungarians began growing varieties of the red pepper paprika in Szeged in southern Hungary. Cultivated in this rich soil and sunny climate, the peppers became so sweet that they bore no resemblance to either their Spanish pimento or their Turkish heritage. Paprika became uniquely, sweetly, Hungarian.

An Emerging Cuisine

The 1700s saw the rule of the Habsburgs, which led to the establishment of the dual monarchy of the Austro-Hungarian Empire in 1867. The Austrians were influenced by German and French cuisine and the preparation methods of the aristocracy. The nobility favored seasoning beef with pepper and poultry with nutmeg.[1] Hot and spicy Hungarian cooking was considered the food of peasants, and the vigorous use of paprika and hot peppers was minimized in favor of the delicately flavored cream and butter sauces of the French. However, the quality and unmatched flavor of Hungary's meat and produce were so extraordinary that the Habsburgs' royal court used Hungary as its pantry.

Baking guilds in both Austria and Hungary existed for every conceivable bread and pastry specialty. The two capitals rivaled each other in perfecting pastry as an art form. The Viennese enriched Hungarian taste sensations with the copious use of whipped cream, chocolate and sugar in their pastry and tortes. Strudel, *rétes*, was a Hungarian invention derived from Turkish *baklava*. Hungarian ingenuity was displayed in varied fillings. The excellent taste and property of Hungarian flour, which allowed the dough to be pulled to translucent thinness, defined its superb quality, transforming strudel into one of the world's best-loved desserts.

"The result of the Viennese influence was that after learning and perfecting the new techniques of food preparation styles, the Hungarians again put their creative mark on them, and their cooking became more varied and enjoyed broader appeal internationally,"[2] wrote Károly Gundel, Hungarian restaurateur and author of several Hungarian cookbooks.

1. Halász, Zoltán. *Hungarian Paprika Through the Ages* (Budapest: Corvina Press, 1963)
2. Gundel, Károly. *Hungarian Cookery Book: 140 Hungarian Specialities* (Budapest: University Printing House, 1969)

It was a French chef who thrust Hungarian cooking onto the world stage. The distinguished place of chicken *paprikás* and beef *guylás* in world cuisine is owed to Georges Auguste Escoffier, whose extraordinary talent popularized Hungarian dishes in the Grand Hotel in Monte Carlo in 1879. With a deft hand, he introduced paprika imported from Szeged into his cooking and thus to the upper class, the aristocracy, royalty and all of Western Europe, drawing culinary attention to its homeland. As a result, in the late 1800s paprika regularly appeared as an ingredient in cookbooks. And though French cooking styles prevailed in Budapest, the villagers continued their zestily seasoned cooking traditions possibly reflecting Asian influence or merely because they preferred more spice.

The Hungarian Mystique and the Good Life

In the 19th century, national pride grew and a political, literary and cultural revival ensued. Both Budapest, the capital, and the Hungarian countryside developed a reputation for the good life, and good food played a major role.

Cosmopolitan Hungarian chefs and confectioners raised the standards of the cuisine overall. The capital's elegantly lavish and lively coffeehouses catered to the intelligentsia, the literati and the "glitterati," serving up exquisitely decorated sweets, tortes and strong coffee at these meetings of minds. The clothing of beautiful women and fashionably dressed city dwellers rivaled Parisian couture. Budapest, as a stop on the Orient Express for transcontinental travel, remained prominent in the public eye.

Yet Hungary remained something of a mystery, owing, in part, to a language that insulated its speakers from the surrounding countries. Unlike the Indo-European languages spoken throughout the Continent, Hungarian is derived from the Finno-Ugric language group, which is different in both vocabulary and grammatical structure. Akin only to Finnish, Lapp, Estonian and certain Siberian dialects, it is spoken by only about 2 percent of the world's population (about 4 percent of the U.S. population).[3] It was and is fiercely preserved. In 1844, Magyar became Hungary's official language, eclipsing German and the Latin tongues. What the language veiled, the lifestyle celebrated.

Beyond the city, shepherds, travelers and villagers were drawn to the countryside inn-and-tavern culture for company, hospitality, good food and drink. Writers, journalists and politicians followed, popularizing

3. Lewis, M. Paul (editor). *Ethnologue: Languages of the World*, sixteenth edition (Dallas, Tex.: SIL International 2009.) Online version: http://www.ethnologue.com and 2000 U.S. Census

the culture and the high-spirited good times there. The music, dancing, singing and handicrafts at the inns were as colorful as the red spice seasoning in the food. Adding to the mystique were the exotic, fortune-telling gypsies and gypsy fiddlers – violinists – whose melodies reflected the strong emotions of the people. Couples danced the *csárdás*, which began slowly and built to a fast tempo as the dancers whirled to syncopated

rhythms. Beautiful Hungarian girls favored richly embroidered, colorful clothes; men donned *szur* cloaks with elaborate metalwork closures. Ornamentation by craftsmen and -women was evidenced in elaborately carved wood furnishings and door posts, hand-painted pottery and dishes and embroidered table coverings. It all added to the inviting nature of inns and the visitors' dining experience. In Hungary, it is said that "art is life" and art is everywhere – further epitomizing the joy of living. All played to the vibrancy, festivity, love, laughter and zest for life, which was irresistible to foreign visitors and made tales of Hungarian travels worth telling.

From Cauldron to Melting Pot

When Hungarians began to arrive in America (see page 212), it was with the hopes of making money and eventually returning to the homeland. Like their hearts, their cooking remained true to the Old Country. They would adapt their cooking to the availability of ingredients and seasonings that went into their American stovetop "kettles."

Flavorful, fresh produce that instills a deep sense of comfort marks the essence of any really good food. Anyone who is passionate about eating recognizes and appreciates quality. Accustomed to their regional tastes and to having fresh, locally grown food at hand, the immigrants (many of whom had come from farming backgrounds and had a fondness for gardening) planted urban backyard vegetable gardens. Herbs, commonly wild in the Hungarian countryside, found their place in cultivated gardens for fresh harvest. Until city laws prevented it, many raised chickens too. Hungarian butchers specialized in cuts of meat familiar to Old World tastes and suited to Old World preparation methods.

The quest for freshness, complex flavors and ethnic variety in meals defines America's culinary "melting pot." Mingled flavors are no less global than those fused by Hungarians over centuries. Eager to experiment with flavors and ingredients, Americans distinct regional differences draw on the offerings of local farmers' markets, the expertise of celebrity chefs, and a rainbow of ethnic restaurants.

While Hungarians still find use for the nostalgic cauldron, Hungarian-Americans have replaced them with slow-cookers, just as they have sped up the flattening of noodle dough with pasta machines. Yet a few time-honored traditions remain in pursuit of flavor: walnuts are best hand-ground just before use, and homemade noodles freshly hand-cut or rolled as for *csiga* are unrivaled. As Americans mix culinary influences, traditional Hungarian dishes may be refashioned in presentation or flavor exchange – a spicy *lecsó* might be used as a salsa-like dip for tortilla chips, or plain white vinegar may be replaced by fancier flavored versions. The transition by both Hungarians and Americans to more healthful cooking led to the replacement of lard, first with bacon fat and later with oil, and to the substitution of sour cream with low-fat versions. Some say such substitutions compromise the original flavors, but they do yield a lighter, healthier fare.

Retaining Authentic Flavors

The recipes that follow reflect a somewhat Americanized style of Hungarian village cooking from the northern part of Hungary, the Borsod-Abaúj-Zemplén regions. Some national "city" recipes appear too. Care was taken to select recipes that retain the flavors taught by parents and grandparents from memory. Rather than relying on the exact measurements of cookbooks, these recipes reflect the Old World cook's mantra, "until it looks/feels/tastes right" – a testimony of their authenticity and proof that Hungarian cooking is characterized by everyday ingredients prepared simply. The essential flavors that comprise the distinctive qualities of the cuisine follow. We invite you to recreate the memorable flavors of your ancestry if you are Hungarian or to experiment with these recipes if you're new to our culture. We hope you will find that they are *nagyon finom* – really delicious!

The paprika growing season begins with seed germination in March, plants set in fields in May and harvesting by hand during September. Hungary's many hot, dry sunshine-filled summer hours, alternating rainfalls, rich fertile soil, the growers know-how and God's blessing yield good harvests.

Kalocsa

Szeged

Unmatched in quality, Hungary's paprika is considered the world's finest in both color and flavor.

Paprika growing is the domain of two cities in the south of Hungary: Szeged, along the Tisza river and Kalosca, along the Danube River. The pinnacle of growing, cultivating and processing evolved from their paprika mastery over generations.

Famous Hungarian puppet star and hero, Jancsi Paprika, has appeared in travelling shows since the early 19th century and even in Hungarian Opera. The joker sports a paprika-shaped hat and in spite of an occasional burst of his "hot" temper, has a kind and generous heart.

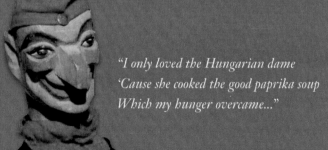

*"I only loved the Hungarian dame
'Cause she cooked the good paprika soup
Which my hunger overcame..."*

Paprika

Paprika is a red, powdered spice made from mild red peppers (Capsicum annuum L.) and is used for its sweet warmth, depth, flavor, color and aroma.

The peppers are grown, hand harvested and strung into garlands to dry throughout the Szeged and Kalosca regions. Peppers from each season's harvest are graded and ground into the spice. Grinding releases the aroma and flavorful oils.

Available in grades ranging from delicate to hot, paprika's beautiful hue varies from bright orange-red to deep, dark crimson. (See chart on the next page.)

To garner the best flavor, purchase Hungarian Szeged or Kalocsa paprika. Commercial paprika mixes less expensive and less flavorful grades.

Flawless paprikas are strung together to dry in the warm sun. They are the chimes of the countryside as they dry, clacking in the gentle winds.

The spice

Paprika combines with virtually every other flavor element. Added to oil, or other fat (traditionally lard) causes the flavor and aroma to bloom. To achieve perfect aroma, color and taste, paprika must not be cooked over high heat; it burns easily which causes it to become bitter, turn brown and ruin the dish. When cooked over low heat, paprika's sugars are released and caramelize slightly, blending with other flavors to develop the character of the dish.

To garnish a dish with color, or as the Hungarians say, "make it a feast for the eyes," paprika may be sprinkled over a dish just before serving.

All recipes that include paprika among the ingredients in this book use sweet Hungarian paprika – Noble Rose – typically packaged in a tin.

13

Paprika Grades

While washing, drying and grinding the paprika is a technological science, the matter of grading the year's harvest relies on human expertise.

A national panel of paprika experts evaluate the taste, color, aroma and pungency to determine which of the seven standard grades best suit the harvest.

Paprika Grades	Qualities	Use
Exquisite delicate Special Quality *Különleges*	Best quality, flawless Hand selected Rich, bright red color Very mild No aftertaste Silky texture Very finely ground	Most delicate; Absolutely no capsaicin; no spice Excellent aroma For seasoning and color
Delicate Gourmet *Csípősmentes csemege*	Strong, bright color More pronounced sweet pepper flavor Medium coarse	Good choice for paprika sauces Rich flavor
Mild Gourmet *Csípős csemege*	Light red Aromatic Finely ground	Slight pungency
Noble sweet *Édesnemes*	Bright red Sweet Medium coarse	Popularly used in Hungarian dishes; most common export in U.S. Slightly pungent
Semi sweet *Félédes*	Light trace of heat Medium coarse and pungent	Pungent, but not hot; a blend of mild and pungent
Rose *Rózsa*	Less red, pale color More heat-spicy Medium coarse	Hot, without being bitter Strong aroma
Hot *Erős*	Pungent and bitter Coarse Brown-orange color	Very hot; use in small quantities, Mixed with other grades for color and depth of flavor
Paprika Paste	**Qualities**	**Use**
Erős Pista (Jar)	Hot, coarse	Stews and soups
Édes Anna (Jar)	Sweet	Stews and soups
Piros Arany (Tube)	Sweet, creamy Mild or sweet	Sandwich condiment or garnish
Storage: Paprika will keep for 2 years if stored in a cool, dark place.		

To your health

Paprika and all hot peppers and their antioxidants are touted for their health benefits. Hungarians have demonstrated this both through research and folkloric medicine.

In the 1930's, Albert Szent-Györgyi validated the high levels of vitamins contained in paprika, specifically vitamins A and C and to a lesser extent, B1, B2. Paprika is the plant world's richest source of Vitamin C. It contains seven times as much as citrus juice. Its vitamin A content exceeds that of carrots. The strength of the A vitamin may explain why there was success in using a tea made from the paprika peppers to treat night blindness or bronchitis and prevent respiratory tract infections. The combination of the vitamins may also explain why the peasants, who often subsisted on bacon, bread and paprika, remained remarkably healthy in spite of lack of nutrition. It stimulates circulation insuring a nice, rosy glow.

The spice was used to fight infection on cuts, sprinkled on the wound in the absence of iodine in the fields. Paprika plasters were used to treat boils. Brandy seasoned with paprika (paprika palinka) was used to treat fevers associated with malaria in the late 19th century and later became the Plains dwellers favorite "medicine" for treating any illness from fever to flu. Not only was that remedy used throughout Hungary but in the Balkans as well.

Capsaicin is the substance that creates pungency in all peppers. Originally quite hot, it is a relative of the cayenne pepper. Paprika exhibits

a variety of pungencies remaining milder than chili powder.

Peppy paprika powers many a palate: it stimulates the appetite and promotes healthy digestion.

Growing paprika

Hungary provides only 10% of the world's paprika. Since it is regarded as the finest, it commands a higher price. (Spain, Israel, India, South America and Texas and California in the United States also grow paprika commercially.) Smoked Spanish paprika bears no resemblance to the mild Hungarian variety. Several U.S. seed companies sell Hungarian paprika seeds if you care to grow your own.

15

Flavor Trinity

The harmony of flavors found in Hungarian cooking begins with the three ingredient combination of fat + onions + paprika.

THIS BASE FOR MANY RECIPES IS ENHANCED BY THE RELEASE OF FLAVORS FROM MEATS OR VEGETABLES, CREATING A VARIETY OF DISHES. THE LEVEL OF ADDITIONAL SEASONING COMPLEMENTS THOSE FLAVORS.

The flavor trinity is created in three steps:

1 A fat (oil, butter, shortening or lard) is heated gently. Into it, add chopped or sliced onions and cook until they appear a translucent, pale, golden yellow, caramelizing the onions.

2 Remove the pan from the heat and add the paprika, sprinkling it over the onions. The warmth of the onions releases the flavor of the paprika, sweetening the dish and creating a mouth-watering aroma.

3 Add meat, vegetables and other seasonings, stirring to envelop them in the mixture and blend them into the base to develop the characteristic rich Hungarian flavors.

Onion

vöröshagyma

Onions are a pervasive flavor in Hungarian cooking. Many dishes rely on the initial step of cooking and stirring the onion in fat or oil, adding paprika followed by the other ingredients.

Yellow or white onions are used with a preference for the sweeter, milder yellow varieties. The degree of pungency of an onion may alter the amount used in a recipe. Low and slow heat ensures that the onions do not burn and is the key to converting the onions' sulphur compounds to sugar, rendering a sweet onion flavor.

Many believe the fat in which the onions are cooked makes a distinctive difference in the dish. Rendered lard was preferred for many years because of its distinct taste and availability. Bacon fat is sometimes used as a substitute. Healthier oils such as canola or olive oils are used today.

Onions can be seasoned with paprika, dill, marjoram, parsley or thyme or studded with cloves in roasts and soups.

Peppers

paradicsompaprika és bogyiszlói

"Paprika" refers not only to the red spice, but also to a complete range of peppers. Most recipes that call for peppers can include varieties from sweet to hot in combination.

The yellow-to-red Hungarian hot banana peppers are eaten fresh, cooked or pickled.

Mild, sweet or medium hot large green and red peppers are typically served stuffed or added to stewing dishes.

Tiny bright fiery-hot red cherry peppers are served along side meals as a condiment.

The hot and very hot peppers should be added judiciously to increase the fire in dishes such as lecsó. A word of warning: very hot peppers have been the ruin of many a dish, so know the heat of a pepper before adding.

17

Parsley &
Parsley Root

*petrezselyem és
petrezselyemgumós*

*Though known for its mildness
and ability to blend with
many herbs, parsley is used to
punctuate the color of a dish
and provide a clarity, freshness
and a crisp, mildly peppery
accent. Both curly and flat
leaf varieties are used.
Parsley is rich in vitamin B
and minerals.*

*Parsley root has always
been popular in Hungarian
cooking, lending itself to long-
simmering cooking methods.*

*Specific varieties are grown for
their whitish roots. The root is
harvested in the autumn of a
two-year old plant. It imparts a
flavor that adds more depth
and is more aromatic than
parsley leaves. Add it to soups,
stews and sauces where its
flavor is best released through
liquids. It pairs especially well
with other root vegetables.*

Marjoram

marjoránna

*Marjoram, a savory herb,
enhances meats and accents
to stuffings and dumplings.*

*Though marjoram and oregano
are from the same family,
oregano is typically not used
in Hungarian cooking.*

*Marjoram's savory earthiness
is best used fresh, added near
the end of cooking to retain
its flavor. Dried leaves deliver
a stronger taste so a smaller
quantity should be used.
Marjoram and paprika
are a perfect marriage of
seasoning flavors.*

18

Dill

kapor

Fresh dill, dried dill weed and dill seed deliver a delightful tang. Its clean, aromatic, herbal qualities add piquancy to meat, fish and vegetables including potatoes, cucumbers and cabbage and sauces. Dill leaves complement cottage cheese.

Dill seed is fundamental in pickles and pickling spices. Seeds can be used in breads.

A member of the parsley family, dill grows under a variety of conditions and its large feathery fronds are a lovely addition to any garden.

Dill has been used for centuries as a soothing digestive.

Caraway

köménymag

From the parsley and carrot family, caraway seed is used to season beef or pork, to accentuate vegetables and to add texture and flavor breads, especially rye bread.

Caraway seeds have a warm aroma, with an earthy, nutty bold, slightly minty-licorice taste.

Dill and caraway are frequently interchangeable.

Paired with meat and cabbage, caraway seed aids in digestion. Seeds are also used to flavor cheese, potatoes, carrots, onions and sausage.

19

Poppy Seed

mákszem

Poppy seed roll – kalács – is
a traditional treat at Easter,
Christmas and special events.
The thick, dark spirals of
poppy seed filling contrast the
white yeast dough and, in
combination, release their nutty
flavor. Poppy seed cakes are also
enhanced by the addition of
orange or lemon zest.

Fresh, loose slate-blue seeds are
sold by the pound at specialty
markets, ground for homemade
pastry fillings. Pre-made,
canned, sweetened fillings may
also be used.

Though introduced by the
Turks, Hungarians made good
use of the seeds.

Poppy seeds dot noodle dishes to
make nice a light lunch.

Poppy seed can be flavored
with lemon juice or zest,
allspice, cloves, cinnamon,
ginger or nutmeg.

Fruit

gyümölcs

The exceptional sweetness of
fruits grown in the Hungarian
soil created a predisposition
for those flavors in America.
Apples, apricots, peaches,
plums, sweet and sour
cherries, raspberries, pears and
currants were used as desserts,
preserves, in pastry fillings
and extracted to make fruit
syrups drizzled on cakes, mixed
into buttercream frostings or
used to flavor sodas. Dried
fruits are often stewed with
cloves, cinnamon and lemon for
desserts. Honey sweet melons
stood alone as a cooling dessert.

The sweet apricots from the
Great Plain (in a district
of Kecskemét) produce an
excellent apricot brandy;
Szamát produces plum brandy.
Brandy-soaked fruits are also
used at the center of chocolate-
covered marzipan candies
from almonds grown above
Lake Balaton.

Lemon zest and lemon juice
spark a subtle hint of flavor in
cheese fillings, doughs or
pancakes where cheese or
fruit or nut fillings are used.

Vinegar

ecet

So prevalent are vinegar and
sour cream in Hungarian
cooking that when the first
Hungarian cookbook was
published in 1695, it already
documented their common use.

Hungarians splash vinegar
into bean and potato soups and
use it with or without oil
as dressings for cucumbers,
cabbage, tomatoes, beans and
potatoes. Sliced vegetables
dressed in vinegar complement
the main dish and lighten the
heaviness of the savory dishes.

Pickles are a popular meal
accompaniment. Vinegar is
used to pickle hot Hungarian
banana or cherry peppers,
cucumbers, carrots, cauliflower
and other vegetables. Pickling
not only extends shelf life of a
variety of raw vegetables, but
it preserves juices and benefits
of the vitamin content while
providing balance and flavor to
the meal.

White vinegar is the usual
choice. Clear, flavored vinegars,
such as tarragon vinegar,
champagne vinegar, rice or
rice wine vinegar can add a
modern twist.

Sour Cream

tejfel

The creamy richness of sour
cream is found in many
Hungarian dishes. Soups are
made velvety by its addition;
sauces are thickened and
mellowed; vegetables are
cooled and enveloped; pastry
is enriched by its presence.
Sour cream is also served
as a condiment.

Its high fat content is identical
to cream but with the addition
of a live culture which gives it
its characteristic tang.

Low-fat or no fat sour cream
may be substituted as healthier
alternatives.

Sour cream will curdle if it
reaches a boiling point so it
must be tempered. Some of the
cooking liquid should be added
to the sour cream before it is
added to the dish, near the end
of the cooking time. It must
be stirred constantly and
briskly when added. A spoon
of flour added to the sour
cream also reduces the risk
of curdling by further
stabilizing the ingredients.

21

Walnuts

dió

Native to Hungary, tall, shade-giving walnut trees populate the hillsides. Their easy availability affords walnuts the premier position of nuts in Hungarian baking.

Fresh walnuts yield the most flavor and the least loss of essential walnut oil. The tradition of making nut rolls, (kalács) or nut filled pastries, (kifli) begins with hand-cracked walnuts. Their high oil content keeps fillings moist. The nuts are also traditionally ground in a hand grinder which is more gentle on the nuts than blenders or food processors which create heat and bitterness. Easily cracked, thin shelled walnuts are preferred.

At Christmas time, walnuts were wrapped in aluminum foil and hung from Christmas trees as both ornament and later, an unwrapped treat. Marzipan was made with walnuts instead of the usual almonds.

Long-lived walnut trees are a traditional symbol of optimism – many future generations will enjoy the nuts.

In 2002 the First Hungarian Reformed Church of Cleveland planted many walnuts trees on church grounds. The trees' lineage is from the Carpathian mountain region in Hungary.

A Canadian monk sought out the trees on high, cold mountains and brought back cuttings to propagate them in North America, hence continuing this symbolic tradition.

Flavor Accents

Cinnamon	*fahéj*
Cloves	*szegfűszeg*
Ginger	*gyömbér*
Horseradish	*torma*
Mustard	*mustár*
Tarragon	*tárkony*
Thyme	*kakukkfű*
Saffron	*sáfrány*
Black peppercorn	*borsszem*

másikíz

The flavors listed to the right appear to a lesser extent, serving as accent flavors. From Asian roots and French, Italian and Austrian-German influences, Hungarians' use of herbs and spices is quite varied.

The pastry spices are cloves and cinnamon.

The Mediterranean herbals – tarragon, thyme and rosemary – are the result of the French and Italian court infusions.

"…strong spices and seasonings such as paprika, pepper, saffron, and ginger also bears the imprint of Asian influence."[4]

Pungent horseradish supplies proper zing to boiled and roasted meats. Horseradish root originally grew wild in Eastern Europe and was later cultivated for its intensity and somewhat sweet peppery flavor.

Magyar tribes rubbed black pepper in abundance on meats to preserve them during transport over the Great Plain.

4. Sisa, Stephen, *The Spirit of Hungary: A Panorama of Hungarian History and Culture* (New Jersey: Vista Books, 1990)

Grace

Come Lord Jesus,
   be our guest,
Let Thy gifts to us
   be blessed.
      Amen.

Martin Luther
1483-1546

Jövel Jezus,
   légy vendégünk,
Áldd meg,
   amit adtál nékűnk.
      Ámen.

Luther Marton
1483-1546

Hungarian Beef Goulash Soup – *Guylásleves*, page 33

SOUP

Ham and Bean Soup with
Farina Dumplings - *Bableves és
nokedli,* page 41

HUNGARIAN SOUPS ARE SO FILLING AND FLAVORFUL THAT
THEY MAY BE SERVED AS MEALS AS WELL AS APPETIZER
COURSES. A GREAT VARIETY OF MEAT, VEGETABLE AND FRUIT
SOUPS, BOTH HOT AND COLD, PROVIDES SEASONAL DIVERSITY.
LONG, SLOW COOKING IS THE KEY TO EXTRACTING THE
ESSENTIAL FLAVORS AND LETTING THE INGREDIENTS SHINE.
MANY HEARTY SOUPS ARE THICKENED WITH A ROUX (*RÁNTÁS*)
OR WITH SOUR CREAM. LIGHTER SOUPS USUALLY PRECEDE
HEAVIER MEALS. A SPLASH OF VINEGAR ADDED TO A THICK
SOUP DELIVERS TANG. LARGE OR SMALL NOODLE SQUARES,
THIN NOODLE STRANDS, *CSIGA* (NOODLES ROLLED ON A
GROOVED BOARD) OR DUMPLINGS ARE ADDED FOR BODY. GOOD
BREAD IS AN ESSENTIAL ACCOMPANIMENT.

Asparagus Soup

Spárgaleves

A creamy, spring soup, this recipe utilizes the entire tender stalk of asparagus.

1-1/2 to 2 pounds asparagus, ends discarded

1-1/2 cups chicken broth

1-1/2 cup heavy cream or half-and-half

1-1/2 tablespoons minced scallion

2 tablespoons butter

3 tablespoons flour

Salt and pepper, to taste

1 Place asparagus in saucepan and cover with broth. Cover and simmer until very tender, about ten minutes.

2 Purée in blender and pour into a quart container, should be about 1 to 1-1/2 cups of purée. Add enough cream to make 3 cups.

3 In saucepan, melt butter; add onion and cook over low heat, stirring, until soft. Blend in flour and continue cook about a minute.

Gradually mix in asparagus purée mixture. Cook and stir until soup bubbles and thickens.

Serves 4-6

Ethel Kardar

Bean Soup "Jokai Style"

Jókai bableves

The namesake of this soup is the famous and prolific Hungarian novelist, Mór Jókai, who loved this soup (but without the vegetables)!

1 smoked pork shank, well washed

1/2 pound dried beans, such as navy beans or two 12 ounce cans of beans, drained with liquid reserved

3 to 4 carrots, peeled and sliced

3 parsnips, peeled and sliced

1 teaspoon paprika

1 tablespoon salt, optional

1 teaspoon whole black peppercorns

1/2 cup sour cream

1 onion, finely chopped

1 clove garlic, peeled and crushed

2 tablespoons shortening

2 tablespoons flour

2 quarts cold water

1 tablespoon vinegar

1/2 pound smoked *kolbász*, optional

Salt and pepper, to taste

1 Place shank in a small soup pot with the dried beans, if using, and cover with water and leave to soak several hours at room temperature or overnight, in refrigerator.

2 Drain and cover with fresh water. Add the carrots, parsnips, garlic and black peppercorns. Simmer over low heat, covered about 45 minutes to one hour, until the pork and beans are tender. If using canned beans, add to broth during last ten minutes of cooking to heat through. Bean liquid may be added as needed to flavor or thin the soup.

Rántás:

3 In a small pan, cook the onion in shortening or oil, stirring frequently. Add flour, continue stirring until the mixture is golden brown. Sprinkle with paprika and dilute mixture with a glass of water. Stir rapidly and add smooth mixture to soup. Add vinegar and boil for 4 to 5 minutes.

4 Pour sour cream into tureen and pour soup on top, stirring constantly as soup is added to ensure sour cream incorporates smoothly

Serves 6-8

In memory of Rt. Rev. Dr. Stephen Szabo

Fresh Green Bean Soup

Friss zöldbableves

Fresh green or wax beans, though available year around, are best in this soup at the peak of harvest.

5 cups water

1 pound fresh green beans, cleaned and cut in even pieces

1/2 teaspoon salt

2 tablespoons butter or lard

2 tablespoons flour

1/2 pint sour cream

4 slices bacon, cut in small pieces

2 tablespoons onion, finely chopped

1/2 teaspoon paprika

2 medium potatoes, boiled and cut in cubes, optional

Fresh dill sprigs, optional

1 tablespoons vinegar + 2 teaspoon sugar, optional

Salt and pepper, to taste

1 Cook the green beans in salted water until tender, about 5 to 7 minutes.

2 In soup pot, melt butter or lard; add flour and stir until golden. Add a half cup of water; stir until smooth. Add cooked beans, liquid and potatoes if using.

3 Simmer for a few minutes, then add sour cream and stir until smooth.

4 Fry the bacon until crisp and drain on paper towels. Add onion to bacon fat and cook, stirring for a few minutes until softened. Stir in paprika. Add mixture to the bean soup.

5 Ladle into bowls and garnish with crisped bacon or dill sprig.

Variation

• For a sweet-sour flavor, add the sugar and vinegar.

Serves 4-6

Ethel Kardar

Red Bean Soup

Pirosbableves

This hearty, vibrantly-colored soup has smoky overtones from the ham or kolbász.

1 pound dry
red kidney beans

3 quarts water with
ham hock – or –
1 pound smoked
kolbász

1 large onion,
chopped

2 cups tomato juice

1/4 cup white vinegar

2 tablespoons
shortening

2 tablespoons flour

2 cups water

Salt and pepper,
to taste

1 Soak beans 8 hours, or overnight. Drain. Place drained beans in soup pot with ham hock or *kolbász* and cover with cold water. Add onion and simmer about 1½ hours or until meat is tender.

2 Add tomato juice and vinegar, if desired.

3 In frying pan, melt shortening. Add flour and brown. Add water and stir until smooth. Whisk into soup. Simmer for a few minutes.

Variation

• Substitute three 12-ounce cans of kidney beans, drained, with liquid reserved instead of dried beans. Reduce cooking time to 45 minutes. Add beans last ten minutes to heat through. Bean liquid may be added to flavor soup, if desired.

Serves 10-12

Brenda Rohaly,
in memory of Mrs Nicholas Rohaly, Sr.

Beef Soup & Vegetable Dinner

Marhahús leves és főzelék

Meat and vegetables are commonly removed from the broth and served as a second course after the soup with a good loaf of Hungarian bread.

3 pounds beef for soup, washed

2 round bones, washed

1 large onion, peeled

3 to 5 potatoes, peeled

6 carrots, peeled

6 stalks of celery

1 green pepper, cored

4 parsley roots with greens, root peeled

1 small wedge of green cabbage

1 kohlrabi

2 tablespoons salt

1/2 teaspoon black pepper

5 quarts water

Cooked noodles

1 Place beef and bones into a 6 quart soup pot. Add cold water to cover, up to 1 inch from top of pot. Bring to a boil, reduce to a simmer. Skim all foam from top using a strainer. Continue skimming until all foam is removed, about 30 minutes. Add salt and pepper, cover and simmer over medium heat about 1½ to 2 hours.

2 Add all vegetables except potatoes and continue simmering, covered, for another hour. Add potatoes and simmer 30 minutes.

3 When soup is done, remove beef and vegetables and place in serving dish. Strain soup and ladle over cooked noodles in soup bowls. Serve beef and vegetables on a platter with mustard or horseradish as a condiment.

Serves 10-12

Elaine Galgany

Hungarian Beef Goulash Soup

Gulyás leves

This Hungarian favorite was originally made in a round bottom kettle with a handle that hung over a fire. A thicker version is a stew called gulyáshús.

1-1/2 pounds beef chuck roast, cut in 1-inch cubes

2 tablespoons shortening

1 tablespoon paprika

1 small onion, minced

3 carrots, chopped

2 stalks of celery, chopped 1/4-inch

2 sprigs of parsley

2 pounds potatoes, cubed

2-1/2 quarts water

Salt, to taste

1 In a soup pot, melt shortening over medium heat and stir and cook the onion until translucent. Add salt and beef and paprika, browning beef on all sides. Add just enough water to barely cover beef and simmer on low heat, covered, for one hour. Add water if necessary to avoid scorching.

2 Add carrots, celery, parsley and at least 2 quarts of water and simmer until vegetables are almost cooked through, about 45 minutes to one hour. Add potatoes and cook another 30 minutes, until potatoes are cooked through.

Variations

• 1 chopped tomato may be added before end of cooking time or a spoon of tomato paste may be used to thicken soup.
• 1 or 2 parsley roots, chopped may be added with carrots.
• 2 sliced green peppers may be added with carrots.
• 1/2 teaspoon caraway seed maybe added with the onion.

Serves 4-6

This classic soup can also be reduced further to become stew by using less water.

In memory of Betty Lengyel Galgany

33

Caraway Seed Soup

Köménymag leves

A peasant soup made of simple ingredients maximizes an essential flavor. Sometimes called betegleves *(sick soup) because caraway eases digestion. It is a good first course for a stuffed cabbage dinner.*

1/3 cup butter (or lard or bacon drippings)

1/3 cup flour

1 tablespoon caraway seeds

1-1/2 quarts water

1 tablespoon salt

1/2 teaspoon paprika

1 Melt fat in large soup pot with tight-fitting lid. Add caraway seed, stirring constantly until golden brown. Add flour and stir to make a dark *rantás*. Do not burn. Remove from heat.

2 Gradually add water and salt, stirring constantly. Return to heat and bring to boil, stirring constantly. Cover and simmer 15 to 20 minutes. Pour through sieve.

Variations

• Add 2 well beaten eggs, whisk into simmering soup cooks to make lacy shreds.

• Just before serving, mix in 3/4 cup heavy cream.

• Add 1 cup chopped onion with caraway seed.

• Serve with garlic- or buttered-flavored croutons or chunks of toasted bread.

Serves 4-6

Barbara Rayer

Cauliflower Soup

Karfiolleves

The short cooking time for this soup preserves the natural sweet flavor of the cauliflower.

8 cups whole milk

1/4 cup minced yellow onion

1/4 cup minced carrot

1/4 cup minced celery

2 pound head of cauliflower

1/3 cup sour cream

2 teaspoons kosher salt

1 teaspoon dried tarragon

2 teaspoons ground white pepper

2 tablespoons unsalted butter

1 teaspoon paprika for garnish

1 tablespoon celery leaves for garnish

1 pinch saffron, optional

1 Core and stem the cauliflower. Remove the florets and chop coarsely. Discard stem and core.

2 In a soup pot, melt the butter over medium heat. Add the onion, carrot and celery. Cook and stir until the onion is translucent, about 3 minutes

3 Add the cauliflower and toss briefly with the onion mixture. Add salt, pepper and tarragon and toss again. Add milk and bring to a boil. Immediately reduce to a simmer. Simmer for about 15 to 20 minutes. The cauliflower should retain some texture.

4 Purée half of the soup in batches until smooth and add back into the soup.

5 Place sour cream into a small bowl. Mix in a small amount of the soup liquid and then add in all into the soup. Simmer 2 minutes longer.

6 Serve topped with a few celery leaves and a pinch of paprika.

Variation

• For color and aroma, add a pinch of saffron with the milk and eliminate the tarragon.

Serves 8-10

Mark Shary

Tart Cherry Soup

Cseresznyeleves

1 pound fresh
tart cherries, pitted–
Do not use
canned cherries.

1 teaspoon
confectioner's sugar

1-1/2 quarts water

3/4 cup sugar

Pinch salt

2 tablespoons flour

1 cup sour cream

This is a nice summer soup that can be prepared with fresh cherries at the July harvest. Refreshing, it may be served as a snack or to cleanse the palate for savory flavors in a multi-course meal. Morellos are the variety of sour cherries popular in Hungary and Balaton® Cherries from Michigan in the U.S. Frozen, canned or dried tart cherries are available, but fresh yields the best flavor.

1 In a medium bowl, stir flour, sour cream, salt and confectioners' sugar until smooth.

2 In a medium saucepan, add sugar to water and simmer cherries until tender.

3 Add two spoonfuls of liquid to the sour cream mixture and stir until smooth. Add the mixture to the soup. Simmer for 5 minutes more. Cover and let cool.

Serves 6-8

Violet Sarosi/American Hungarian Foundation

Old-Fashioned Chicken Soup

Csirkeleves

This soup has an elusive aroma and golden yellow color. For robust flavor, the chef cautions not to use a young chicken.

1 stewing hen, 3-1/2 to 4 pounds, quartered

2 cups coarsely chopped carrots

4 celery ribs, chopped

1 small onion, unpeeled studded with 1 clove in root end

1 parsley root or parsnip

1 piece celery root or white or yellow turnip

1 clove garlic

1 tablespoon salt

12 black peppercorns

1/8 teaspoon each mace and nutmeg

1 or 2 saffron threads

1-1/2 to 2 pounds beef or veal bones

1 gallon water

1 tablespoon chopped parsley

1 piece chicken belly fat from cavity of hen*

1 tablespoon sugar

1 tablespoon butter

1 tablespoon finely grated carrot

1 In a large stockpot, place all ingredients through water. Bring to a boil over medium heat. Reduce heat and simmer at least 4 hours. Remove from heat and let the soup stand 30 minutes. Skim off the fat and strain the soup into another pot. Cool the meat and vegetables.

2 Cook and stir the parsley in the chicken fat for 1 to 2 minutes. This will give the soup an intense flavor base. Add the cooked carrots, parsnip or parsley root. Cover and reduce heat to very low, cook 10 minutes. This will heighten the flavor of the vegetables.

3 In a small skillet, heat the sugar slowly until it starts to turn brown. Add the butter and the grated carrot. Stir for 10-15 seconds then remove from heat and dilute with 1/2 cup of chicken soup. Bring it to a rapid boil and strain it through a fine sieve into the soup. This will give a beautiful color to the soup.

4 Remove the chicken skin and bones and cut the meat into chunks. Place the meat and the vegetables cooked with the parsley into a serving dish. Pour the soup over them and serve immediately.

* *Tip*

The belly fat of the chicken is at the end of the breast and around the upper part of the thigh.

Serves 8

In memory of Bill Koteles – his favorite soup; adapted from Chef Louis Szathmary

Kohlrabi Soup

Karalábéleves

Kohlrabi is common to Hungarian gardens and dinner tables. A relative of the cabbage family, its flavor mellows during cooking.

1-1/2 pound meaty veal ribs or neck bones

4 quarts water

1 medium onion, chopped

1 tablespoon butter

1 tablespoon salt

1 tablespoon pepper

1 teaspoon paprika

Pinch of saffron

4 to 5 medium kohlrabi, leaves trimmed off and cut into 1/4-inch slices

4 to 5 carrots, peeled and cut into 1-1/2-inch slices

Rántás

1/4 cup flour and

3 tablespoons butter

1 tablespoon chopped parsley

Farina dumplings

3 eggs

1/2 teaspoon salt

1 cup farina

1 Cook and stir the onions in 1 tablespoon butter until translucent. Set aside.

2 In a large pot, place veal ribs or neck bones in 4 quarts of water; bring to a boil; skim foam from the top; repeat until no foam forms, about 30 minutes.

3 Stir in onions and salt, pepper, paprika and saffron.

4 Simmer about 1-1/2 hours or until veal is almost tender. Add kohlrabi and carrots; cook about 45 minutes longer. Remove bones and discard. Add veal back into the soup.

5 Near the end, make *rántás* in small frying pan: melt 3 tablespoons butter and add the flour; stirring mixture constantly until golden; add chopped parsley and dilute mixture with 1 cup water or soup broth; stirring rapidly until smooth. Add mixture to soup. Stir.

6 Serve with the farina dumplings.

Farina Dumplings

1 Whip eggs in small bowl with salt. Slowly mix in farina until smooth and creamy. Let stand for about 30 minutes.

2 Drop batter from tip of spoon into soup; cook about 20 minutes until tender, depending on size of dumpling.

Serves 6-8

In memory of Elsie Skomski – her mother's recipe

Lentil Soup

Lencseleves

Lentil dishes were common to the Bakony mountain region in Hungary. Lentils are a New Years' Day tradition, thought to bring good luck and riches.

1-1/2 cup dried lentils

Cold water for soaking

Small ham hock

1 garlic clove, peeled

1/4 teaspoon black peppercorns

1 medium onion, chopped 1/4-inch

1 bay leaf

2 cups chopped carrots

1/8 teaspoon pepper

1 Pick over then wash the lentils. Soak overnight.

2 Cook and stir onion in butter until golden.

3 Drain and measure liquid from beans, adding enough cold water to make 2-1/2 quarts. Pour into a soup pot and add ham hock. Tie garlic and peppercorns in a cheesecloth and add to pot with onions, bay leaf and pepper. Cover and simmer 1 hour or, in a slow cooker up to 4 hours.

4 Remove ham and set aside. Remove cheesecloth and bay leaf and discard. Add chopped carrots to the soup and continue simmering until lentils and carrots are tender, about 25 to 35 minutes.

Variation

• Split peas may be substituted for lentils.

• 1 teaspoon tarragon may be added to the cheesecloth flavor bundle.

• Chopped tarragon and celery leaves may be used as garnish

Serves 6

In memory of Olga Kish

Mushroom Soup

Gombaleves

A beautiful golden, translucent soup is accented by paprika and parsley.

1 pound button mushrooms, cleaned and sliced or a variety, see variation below

1 clove garlic, finely chopped

2 tablespoons finely chopped parsley

1 onion, chopped 1/4-inch

3 tablespoons butter

1 teaspoon salt

1 teaspoon paprika

3 tablespoons flour

4 cups chicken stock

1/2 cup sour cream, optional

1 In a two-quart soup pot, melt butter over medium high heat. Add onion and cook, stirring constantly about 2 minutes, stirring. Reduce heat slightly, add garlic and cook and stir 2 minutes more. Mix in mushrooms and parsley and cover. Stir occasionally and continue cooking about 5 to 7 minutes until mushrooms release their liquid.

2 Stir in salt, paprika and flour, stirring to cook flour, about 3 minutes until the flour is completely incorporated into mixture.

3 Add half of the chicken stock and stir until thickened slightly and smooth.

4 Add remaining stock and bring to a boil; immediately reduce heat and simmer about 5 minutes. For a lighter soup, serve immediately or for a richer soup, continue.

5 Add a cup of soup to sour cream and whisk quickly. Add back into soup, stirring to blend.

Variations

• For a more complex mushroom flavor, a variety of mushrooms, such as shiitake, oyster or others may be used. Chanterelle and morel mushrooms, though expensive, are commonly used in Hungary because they grow wild along the Danube.

• Bacon fat imparts a rich, smoky flavor and may be used instead of butter.

Serves 4-6

Mark Shary

Pork Soup & Vegetables Dinner

Sertés húsleves és főzelék

Pork is prominent in Hungarian cooking. It is roasted, fried, used in sausages, pickled and used here in soup.

2-1/2 pounds whole pork loin

2-1/2 tablespoons salt

4 carrots, peeled

4 stalks celery, cut in half

1 large onion, quartered

6 to 8 parsley sprigs

4 quarts water

1 Place water and pork loin in a 6-quart pot with lid. Bring to a boil and skim foam from the top.

2 Add salt and vegetables. Bring to a boil, reduce heat to a simmer for 2-1/2 hours. Pierce pork with fork to make sure it is tender.

3 Serve broth with noodles. Serve vegetables and pork on platter with horseradish as a condiment.

Serves 6-8

Gizella Dienes

Ham & Bean Soup

Bableves

Fresh green beans make this a harvest soup; canned beans are a good winter substitute.

Cottage ham, about 1-1/2 pound

Beans, green or waxed; or can navy beans

2 tablespoons shortening

1/4 cup flour

2 tablespoons chopped onion

1 cup water

1/2 cup sour cream

1 tablespoon flour

1 Place ham in a medium stock pot. Cover with cold water. Bring to a boil and reduce heat. Simmer 60 to 75 minutes, until ham is tender.

2 Add beans; simmer about 30 minutes. Remove ham, cube when cool enough to cut.

3 In saucepan, melt shortening; add onion and cook slowly, stirring, until soft. Slowly blend in flour, stirring until golden. Add water, stirring until smooth. Cook 10 minutes. Add to broth.

4 Mix a tablespoon of flour into sour cream. Add some of the broth to warm the mixture then stir into the soup. Cook over low heat 5 minutes. Add ham. Serve with farina dumplings, see page 92.

41

Potato Soup

Krumplileves

In the spring or summer, add chives and lemon zest or a pinch of fresh marjoram with a grind of black pepper to this timeless comfort soup.

2-1/2 pounds potatoes cubed (about 4 to 5 large, 6 to 7 medium or 10 small potatoes)

3 carrots, sliced into rounds

4 stalks of celery, sliced

1/8 pound bacon, sliced sideways

1 small onion, chopped

4 tablespoons (1/2 stick) butter

1/4 cup flour or more if needed

2 cups whole milk

1/2 cup sour cream

1 teaspoon paprika, or more to taste

Salt, pepper, to taste

Chopped parsley for garnish

1 In a large soup pot, cover the potatoes with water and cook until tender, about 15 to 20 minutes. Coarsely mash potatoes in cooking water.

2 Add carrots and celery to broth and simmer until tender.

3 In a small or medium skillet, fry bacon until crisp. Remove bacon, drain on paper towel and set aside for garnish.

4 Cook the chopped onion in the bacon fat, stirring so as not to burn. Remove onions and add onion to the soup.

5 Melt butter into bacon fat. Slowly add flour and paprika to bacon fat and, stirring constantly to brown nicely. Add milk and stir until smooth and blended. Slowly pour into soup to thicken.

6 Mix a small amount of soup broth into sour cream, slowly to raise the temperature and prevent curdling. Add the sour cream mixture to the soup a little at a time stirring to blend evenly.

7 Season with salt and pepper. Garnish with parsley and bacon.

Variations

• Add a bay leaf to simmering soup.

• Adding a tablespoon of flour to the sour cream will also prevent curdling.

Serves 8

Gladys Uveges

Pumpkin Soup

Tökleves

This richly-flavored creamy white soup is perfect on a crisp autumn day.

1 large green pumpkin (under-ripe)

2 tablespoons butter

1 onion, chopped

1 clove garlic, very finely chopped

1/2 teaspoon paprika

1 cup sour cream

2 tablespoon flour

1 cup hot water

1 teaspoon salt

1 tablespoon chopped fresh dill or 1 teaspoon dried

White or white wine vinegar to taste

1 Cut top off pumpkin; remove and discard seeds. Cut into pieces and shred on grater.

2 Place shredded pumpkin in large saucepan. Add water to cover and salt, bring to a boil and simmer until cooked fork tender, about 10 minutes. Be careful not to overcook or the pumpkin will become mushy.

3 Meanwhile, combine the sour cream and flour in a small bowl. When pumpkin is almost cooked, add a small amount of the hot liquid to the flour mixture then add into the cooking pumpkin, stirring constantly until blended. Keep over very low heat.

4 In a small saucepan or frying pan, melt butter and add chopped onion and garlic. Cook over low heat until the onions are golden. Remove from heat and stir in paprika. Add the onion mixture to the soup. Add dill and serve with good rye bread. A splash of vinegar may be added to taste at serving time.

Variation

• Orange pumpkin may be substituted but cooking time will lengthen.

Serves 6-8

Jerry (and Irene) Takacs

Sauerkraut Soup

Káposztaleves

The essential flavors in this soup combine the tang of the sauerkraut balanced by the richness of the meats.

3 slices bacon

1 medium onion, chopped

1 teaspoon paprika

4 cups water

2 ham hocks smoked

1 green pepper

1 tomato

One 16-ounce can sauerkraut, washed and drained

1 tablespoon flour

1/2 pint sour cream

1/2 pound Hungarian smoked *kolbász*, cut in 1-1/2-inch pieces

1 Brown bacon in Dutch oven or large pot with tight fitting lid. Remove bacon and reserve. Brown onions in bacon drippings until transparent. Add paprika, water, ham hocks, green pepper and tomato.

2 Simmer 1-1/2 hours or until ham is tender. Remove ham hocks and cut ham from bone. Return ham to soup. Add sauerkraut and cook 20 minutes.

3 Combine flour and sour cream and add to soup mixture along with *kolbász*. Bring soup to a simmer and serve hot with additional sour cream on side and crumbled bacon as garnish.

Variation

• Dill and garlic may be used to season.

Serves 4-6

Barbara Rayer

Split Pea Soup

Borsóleves

Simple ingredients become a healthful soup.

1 pound split peas

3 quarts
boiling water

Smoked ham shank
or ham bone

1 onion,
coarsely chopped

1 large carrot,
coarsely grated

2 stalks celery,
thinly sliced

1 Place all ingredients in a large soup pot over medium low heat. Simmer two hours or more stirring occasionally to prevent scorching.

2 Remove shank or bone from soup and let cool. When cooled, remove ham from bone and set aside.

3 Rub soup through a sieve or purée in blender. Put ham into soup and reheat.

Serves 8-10

In memory of Betty Kinkopf

Creamy Tomato Soup

Tejfeles paradicsomleves

Spark this velvety soup with your choice of the essential flavors listed in the variations.

2 pounds potatoes, peeled and cubed,

1 quart water

1 quart tomato juice

3 tablespoons flour

2 tablespoons sour cream

1 pint half-and-half

2 cups milk

Salt, pepper and a little sugar, to taste

1 Cook potatoes in salted water for 15 to 20 minutes, drain and set aside.

2 Pour tomato juice and 1 quart water in large soup pot.

3 In a small bowl, combine flour and sour cream to a smooth paste; add half-and-half and milk slowly; add to tomato juice and bring to a boil, stirring constantly. Cook about 5 minutes; add cooked potatoes and keep cooking until it again comes to a boil. Boil slowly for another 5 minutes. If too thick, add a little more milk.

Variation

• 1/2 teaspoon dry or 1/2 tablespoon fresh marjoram, dill or tarragon may be added during the last 10 minutes of cooking time.

Serves 6-8

Betty Lawrence and Emma Koch,
In memory of Emma Ozsvath

Tomato Cabbage Soup with Pork

Paradicsomos káposztaleves

A hearty and familiar combination of pork and cabbage delivers an abundance of flavor.

1-1/2 pound pork shoulder, boned, trimmed of fat, cubed, rinsed and patted dry

2 large onions, coarsely chopped

3 cloves garlic, chopped

1 teaspoon salt

Pepper, to taste

3 to 4 pound green cabbage, halved, cored and chopped

36 ounces tomato purée

1 cup sugar, plus or minus depending on acidity of tomato

2 cups milk

4 to 5 tablespoons flour

1 In a large soup pot, place pork and bones into a sauce pan and cover with water, 1 inch over pork. Add onion, garlic and salt. Cook about 45 minutes to an hour until pork is tender. Remove pork from broth, reserving liquid and set aside until cool enough to handle. Remove pork from bones and set aside. Discard bones.

2 While pork is cooking, place cabbage in another large pot. Fill pot quarter full with water. Stir and add water if needed to prevent scorching. Cook about 45 minutes until tender.

3 Add tomato purée and pork and liquid from Step 1. Stir in sugar. Pour in milk and stir until mixture comes to a boil and reduce to a simmer.

4 In a small saucepan, ladle 1 cup of the soup and quickly mix in flour to form a smooth paste. Work quickly and pour into soup and return to a simmer for 5 minutes. Soup should be moderately thick. For thicker soup add more flour to 1/4 cup cold water and quickly stir into soup. Soup may be served with a dollop of sour cream.

Serves 8-10

Yolanda Turocy

47

Fresh Vegetable Soup

Zöldségleves

The vegetable variety can change by season; the addition of the cabbage or kohlrabi makes the flavor decidedly Hungarian.

6 to 8 cups vegetables, cleaned, diced or sliced fresh vegetables such as: carrots, celery, green beans, peas, lima beans

2 tomatoes, diced

1 to 2 potatoes, peeled and chopped into cubes

Parsley root with greens

1 small head savoy cabbage, chopped

1 large onion, chopped

3 tablespoons butter or bacon fat

1/4 cup flour

1 tablespoon paprika

Salt and pepper, to taste

1 to 2 quarts beef broth or water

1 In a large stock pot, melt butter or bacon fat and add chopped onion. Cook, stirring, until golden. Add paprika, stir. Mix in vegetables, except savoy cabbage. Continue cooking, stirring occasionally until semi-soft, about 20 minutes.

2 Add cabbage, stir and cook 10 minutes longer; season with salt and pepper. Remove parsley and root and discard.

3 Gradually sprinkle flour on vegetables, stirring constantly. Add broth (or water) to cover vegetables by an inch. Bring to boil, reduce to simmer until thickened, about 10 minutes.

Variations

• A wedge of green cabbage or quartered kohlrabi may be substituted for the savoy cabbage.

• This soup may be served over cooked rice or barley.

Serves 6-8

In memory of Mary Kovach

Zucchini Soup

Cukkínileves

Hungarians use a large squash called vegetable marrow, which may be available in some markets. Abundant zucchini is a delicious alternative.

Zucchini, about 3 pounds, peeled, cut lengthwise, seeds removed, grated on largest holes on grater into ribbons

1 large onion, finely chopped

1/4 pound (1 stick) margarine or butter

Pepper

Paprika

2 cloves of garlic, finely chopped

Marjoram, optional

Salt and pepper, to taste

1-1/2 quarts water, vegetable or chicken stock

1 cup flour

2 eggs

1 cup sour cream, optional

Sugar, optional

1 Salt zucchini, let stand 10 minutes and squeeze out moisture.

2 In a soup pot, melt margarine or butter over medium high heat and add onion. Cook and stir until translucent. Add pepper, paprika, garlic and marjoram, if using. Continue cooking for about five minutes over low heat. Add zucchini.

3 Add stock or water and simmer for 15 to 20 minutes to warm though.

4 Mix flour with eggs to make a paste and add a little water. Gradually stir into the soup to thicken.

5 If desired, add sour cream after soup is thickened.

6 Add sugar to taste, if desired.

Serves 6-8

Margaret Jacob

Fried Pork – *Laci pecsenye*, page 71

MEAT & POULTRY

Fried pork, sausage and
stuffed cabbage – *Laci pecsenye,
kolbász és töltött káposzta*

MEAT PLAYS A PROMINENT ROLE IN HUNGARIAN CUISINE
OWING TO THE NOMADIC ROOTS OF THE MAGYARS, WHO
BROUGHT WITH THEM HARDY CATTLE, SHEEP AND PIGS FOR
BOTH FOOD AND TRADE.[5] PORK IS CLEARLY THE FAVORITE.
"NO OTHER PEOPLE ON EARTH EXCEPT THE CHINESE USE
PORK IN AS MANY WAYS AS HUNGARIANS."[6] LEAN CUTS
OF BEEF OR PORK PRODUCE THE BEST FLAVORS; THE LONG
BRAISING TIMES TYPICAL OF HUNGARIAN COOKING RESULT
IN RICH JUICES THAT MAY BE ENHANCED WITH *RÁNTÁS* OR
SOUR CREAM TO PRODUCE THICK, FLAVORFUL GRAVIES. (GOOD
BREAD IS ESSENTIAL TO SOAK UP EVERY DELICIOUS DROP.)
FINALLY, BLENDS OF SPICES AND THE HIGHEST-QUALITY
PORK YIELD THE PINNACLE SAUSAGE, *KOLBÁSZ.* ADDING RICE
AND LIVER TO GROUND PORK PRODUCES *HURKA* SAUSAGE.
POULTRY'S STARRING ROLE IS CHICKEN *PAPRIKÁS*, DRESSED IN
A VELVETY, SOUR CREAM-PAPRIKA SAUCE.

5. Halász, Zoltán, *Hungarian Paprika Through the Ages* (Budapest: Corvina Press, 1963)
6. Wechsberg, Joseph. *The Cooking of Vienna's Empire* (New York: Time Life Books, 1968.) p. 105

DISH	Pörkölt	Tokány	Paprikás	Gulyás
MEAT	Large cubes of veal, beef, mutton, or game	Thin, long strips of veal, beef, lamb, pork or mixed meat	Cubed or cut chicken or veal	Cubed beef
METHOD	Stew slowly; season with a generous amount chopped onions and paprika; Sear meat to seal edges; add water or stock to barely cover meat; cover and stew; reduce liquid to a rich gravy	Braise meat; season liberally with black pepper, onion, garlic, marjoram Paprika is typically not used; Add very little water during cooking, allowing meat to simmer a in its own juices reducing and intensifying the flavor. The sauce thickens and envelops meat .	Stew poultry/veal; season with chopped onions and paprika; Brown rapidly to seal edges; add water or stock to barely cover meat; simmer covered; finish with sour cream gravy	Simmer as a soup; longer stewing time lengthens gravy
FLAVOR	Garlic; green peppers and/or tomatoes	Bay leaves, parsley root, mushrooms, smoked bacon, ginger and saffron	Caraway, garlic, peppers or carrots	Paprika, green pepper, tomatoes, hot cherry peppers, mushrooms
SERVE WITH	*Nokedli, tarhonya* or homemade noodles	Potatoes; Dollop of sour cream	*Nokedli*/dumplings or cubed potatoes	Potatoes or dumplings
RECIPE	PAGE 59	PAGE 55	PAGE 61, 78	PAGE 33

Beef & Sauerkraut Casserole

Rakott káposzta

A layered dish featuring beef, rice and sauerkraut, and a sour cream-milk mixture between layers.

2 pounds
ground beef

2 pounds sauerkraut,
rinsed and drained

4 tablespoons (1/2
stick) butter or
margarine,
divided

1 cup long grain rice

2 teaspoon salt,
divided

2 cups boiling water

1/4 cup milk

1/2 cup sour cream

1 Melt butter or margarine in large frying pan. Add beef and salt and brown.

2 Cook rice in boiling water for 10 minutes, stirring occasionally. Drain rice and rinse with cold water; drain.

3 Stir milk into sour cream. Rinse sauerkraut slightly and drain. Grease a 12 x 9 x 3-inch glass or noncorrosive baking dish.

4 Line bottom of a baking dish with a third of the sauerkraut. Add half of the ground beef and half of the rice. Dot surface with sour cream. Repeat layers of sauerkraut, beef, rice and sour cream, ending with sauerkraut.

5 Bake at 400° for 40 minutes.

Variations

• Bacon drippings or lard would add more flavor; substitute for butter or margarine.

• For a pork version, see page 73.

Serves 6-8

Betty Rose Galgany

Esterházy Steak

Esterházy rostélyos

Named for Prince Pál Esterházy, this braised steak and vegetable combination can also be prepared by puréeing the vegetables to create the sauce.

2 pound round steak, cut 1-inch thick

1/2 cup flour

2 teaspoon salt

1/2 teaspoon pepper

1/3 cup fat

3 carrots, peeled and sliced

2 small onions, peeled and sliced

1 parsnip, peeled and chopped

1 rib celery, chopped

Gravy

1 tablespoon fat

1 tablespoon flour

1/4 teaspoon salt

Pinch pepper

1 cup broth

1/4 cup dry white wine

1 cup sour cream mixed with 1 teaspoon paprika

1 Pound steak well. Cut steak in serving pieces and dredge with mixture of flour, salt and pepper.

2 Heat fat in skillet and brown steaks on both sides. Remove and set aside. Add vegetables to skillet, reduce heat and cook slowly about 10 minutes. Arrange steaks in 11 x 7 x 1-1/2-inch greased baking dish and spoon vegetables over meat.

3 In the same skillet, heat 1 tablespoon fat, 1 tablespoon flour, salt and pepper until mixture bubbles and is lightly browned. Add broth; bring to boil. Remove from heat and add wine. Pour sauce over vegetables and steak. Cover tightly.

4 Bake at 350° for about 1-1/4 hours or until steak is done. Uncover. Spread sour cream mixture over vegetables and return to oven, uncovered and bake about 15 minutes. Garnish with 1 tablespoon chopped flat-leaf parsley.

Serves 6-8

In memory of Rt. Rev. Dr. Stephen Szabo

Beef Strips Stew

Tokány

Tokány *is characterized by a thick sauce that is the result of the meat braising in its own juices.*

1-3/4 pounds round steak or beef flank, cut into short, thin strips

1 onion (5 ounces), cut into thin strips

1 clove garlic, crushed

1 teaspoon fresh ground black pepper

1 teaspoon marjoram

1/2 teaspoon salt

2 teaspoons tomato paste

3 tablespoons oil

1/2 cup dry white wine or water

1 Fry the onions in oil until golden. Add meat and sear on all sides. Season with salt, pepper and marjoram. Add garlic and wine and stir for 2 to 3 minutes.

2 Cover and let simmer. To prevent scorching, add a little water, if necessary. Add tomato paste when meat is approximately half cooked, about 5 minutes.

3 Cook until meat is tender and gravy is reduced as much as possible to a smooth, brown sauce that envelops the meat.

Serve with *tarhonya*, rice or mashed potatoes and sour pickles.

Serves 4-6

Variation

• Veal, lamb or pork may be prepared in this method.

Liver, Tomato & Onions

Hagymás-májas paradicsommal

Whether liver dumplings, liver with vinegar sauce, liver sausages or liver with onions, Hungarians prepare the much maligned liver deliciously.

1 tablespoon plus 1 teaspoon margarine, divided

1 cup sliced onions, separated into rings

2 medium tomatoes, sliced

1/2 teaspoon marjoram leaves

3 tablespoons flour

1/2 teaspoon salt

Dash pepper

10 ounces calves liver, thinly sliced

Parsley to garnish

1 In a 10 to 12-inch skillet, melt half the margarine. Add onions and cook until tender but not soft. Remove onions from skillet and keep warm.

2 Place tomatoes into same skillet and briefly cook each side. Remove and add to onions. Sprinkle with marjoram.

3 On waxed paper, combine flour, salt and pepper; dredge liver in flour mixture on both sides.

In same skillet heat remaining margarine until bubbly and hot. Add liver and quickly fry, turning once, until juices are released and evaporated.

Do not overcook. Remove to serving plate and top with onion and tomato slices. Garnish with parsley sprigs.

Variation

• Add paprika to the flour mixture as well.

Serves 2-3

In memory of Margie Csolty

Beef Roast with Dill Sauce

Sült marhahús kapormártással

Beef roast takes on a Hungarian personality with caraway, paprika, garlic, onions and dill.

3 to 4 pound beef top round roast, rinsed and patted dry

1/2 teaspoon paprika

3 cloves fresh garlic, thinly sliced

1 teaspoon caraway seed

Salt and pepper, to taste

2 onions, quartered

2 tablespoons shortening or oil

Dill Sauce

2 tablespoons butter

2 tablespoons flour

1/2 teaspoon salt

1/2 cup meat stock

1 tablespoon chopped fresh dill

1/2 cup sour cream

Preheat oven to 350°

1 Season the roast on all sides with salt, pepper, paprika and caraway seed. With a sharp knife, make small cross-shaped incisions about 1/2-inch deep and insert sliced garlic.

2 In a roasting pan, add shortening or oil and onions and any remaining garlic. Brown all sides of the beef and roast for 2 to 3 hours until tender.

3 Serve with horseradish or dill sauce.

Dill Sauce

1 In a heavy saucepan, blend butter, flour and salt over low heat. Stir in beef stock and cook until smooth and thickened.

2 Remove pan from heat, add dill and sour cream and mix.

Variation to the Roast

• Potatoes and carrots may be added to the roast during the last 40 minutes of cooking.

Serves 6-8

American-Hungarian Hamburgers

Fasirt

Hungarians had to have the all-American burger their way.

2 pounds ground sirloin

1/2 pound day-old bread, cubed or crumbled

3 large eggs

1/2 cup milk

1 cup finely chopped onions

1 to 2 teaspoons hot paprika, optional

Green peppers, finely chopped, optional

3 cloves garlic, minced, optional

Salt and pepper, to taste

1 Mix all ingredients. If necessary, add more milk or bread crumbs for mixture to come together.

2 Form patties and grill until cooked through.

Serves 6-8

Dr. Dezso J. Ladanyi

Beef or Pork & Peppers

Pörkölt

This sizzling sauté is a marriage of two classic ingredients. Combine a variety of peppers if you like.

3/4 pound
pork or beef sirloin,
cut into large cubes

2 tablespoons oil

1 large yellow onion,
peeled and sliced thin

3 medium green
peppers, cored,
seeded and cut
into 1/4-inch strips

1 clove garlic, minced

1/2 teaspoon salt

1 tablespoon
paprika

1/2 teaspoon sugar

1 Heat 1 tablespoon oil in large skillet over moderately high heat. Add onion, green peppers and garlic and cook, cover for 3 minutes. Reduce heat to medium and add paprika, salt and sugar; cook partly covered for 10 minutes. Transfer to warm bowl and set aside.

2 Heat remaining oil in skillet over high heat for 1 minute. Add meat and cook, uncovered, stirring frequently for about 5-10 minutes, until browned and cooked through.

3 Return onion and pepper mixture to the skillet and toss until heated through, about 2 minutes. Serve with buttered noodles.

Serves 4

In memory of Margie Csolty

Budapest Chicken Breast

Budapesti csikremell

For a cosmopolitan flair in chicken, this recipe is as rich and appealing as the city that shares its name.

2 large sweet onions

2 tablespoons unsalted butter

1/4 pound parmesan cheese

1/4 pound Swiss cheese

1/2 cup bread crumbs

1/3 cup white wine (Hungarian Szurke Barat, (Grey Friar) preferred

3/4 cup chicken stock

1 teaspoon paprika

1 teaspoon salt

1/4 teaspoon white pepper

6 to 8 boneless, skinless chicken breasts

Preheat oven to 350°

1 Slice onions thinly and cook in butter, stirring until translucent, about 15 minutes.

2 Place one layer of onions in pan that is 2 inches high or less. Season the chicken breasts with salt and pepper and place them in the pan.

3 Mix bread crumbs, cheese(s) and paprika. Sprinkle on top of the chicken breasts.

4 Mix white wine and soup. Pour over the chicken breasts, soaking the bread crumb mixture.

5 Bake in the top third of the oven for 1 hour. Reduce heat to 250° and continue baking for 30 minutes.
Serve with rice or *tarhonya*.

Serves 6-8

Lenke Forgach Magyar

Chicken Paprikas

Paprikás csirke

A thick, sour cream-paprika gravy characterizes this national dish.

3-1/2 to 4 pound chicken, cleaned and washed and cut into 8 serving pieces

2 medium onions, chopped

3 tablespoons fat

1 tablespoon paprika

1-1/2 cup water or chicken broth

1 teaspoon salt

1 teaspoon pepper

2 tablespoons flour

1/2 cup sour cream

1/2 green pepper, seeded, chopped, optional

1/2 tomato, chopped, optional

1 In a dutch oven or large frying pan, cook and stir onion in fat slowly until softened and golden. Remove from heat and stir in paprika and salt, so as not to brown paprika. Add chicken pieces, brown. Mix in green pepper and tomato, if using. Pour water over chicken to cover and simmer until chicken is tender, about 1 hour.

2 In a small bowl, mix flour and sour cream until smooth; add a little of the hot liquid from the chicken into the sour cream mixture, stir and add to pan, stirring to thicken and to develop a nice color, about 2 to 8 minutes on low heat.

3 Serve with dumplings or boiled potatoes and a cucumber vinaigrette salad.

Serves 6-8

In memories of Olga Kish and Julia Molnar

Chicken Fricassee

Csirkebecsinált

This is the Hungarian version of fried chicken which imparts the signature aroma of paprika and onion during the final roasting.

1 chicken fryer, cut in serving pieces, rinsed and dried well

Salt, pepper,

1 cup flour, for dredging

1/2 tablespoon paprika

1 large onion

1/2 cup water

Shortening, for frying

1 Sprinkle chicken with salt and pepper. Mix paprika with flour. Dredge chicken with flour/paprika mixture until all pieces are evenly coated.

2 In a heavy skillet, melt shortening to depth of 1-inch. When fat is moderately hot, 350°, gently add the chicken, being careful not to crowd. Fry until chicken is a golden brown.

3 Remove pieces to a roasting pan. Pour approximately one half cup water into the bottom of the pan. Slice the large onion and place slices between layers of chicken. Cover and roast at 350° until tender, approximately 1 hour.

Serves 4-6

Margaret Palchesko and Betty Palchesko

Giblets & Rice

Ludas Rizs

Even though giblets aren't as popular as they once were, this is a way to use all of the chicken.

1 pound giblets

1 small onion, finely chopped

1 rib celery, chopped 1/4-inch

1 carrot, chopped 1/4-inch

1 cup uncooked rice

1/2 teaspoon salt

1/2 teaspoon pepper

2 tablespoons butter

1 In covered pan, cook giblets in just enough water to cover, until soft, about 10 minutes,

2 Remove, cool and cut into bite sized pieces. Set broth aside.

3 In a baking dish, melt butter and cook and stir rice until butter is absorbed. Mix rice, carrot, celery, giblets, strained broth, salt and pepper. Cover and bake at 350° until rice is tender, at least 1 hour. During baking time, stir rice and add more liquid if necessary to prevent scorching.

Serves 4-6

In memory of Betty Lengyel Galgany

Hungarian Rice & Liver Sausage

Májas hurka

The crispy outside and soft, warm and spicy inside of this sausage is even more delicious if made at home.

Sausage casings

4 pounds long-grained rice

1 pork liver

1 pork heart

2 pork tongues

4 to 5 pounds pork trimmings or fatback

4 to 5 large onions, minced

3/4 cup salt, approximately

1/3 cup black pepper

1 Soak casing in lukewarm water overnight. Rinse several times. Cut into 15-inch lengths.

2 Cook rice until nearly done. Rinse several times in cold water. Drain well. Place in pan large enough to later hold all ingredients.

3 Clean liver, heart and tongues, cook in salted water until done. Pull skin off the tongues after it is cooked. Grind the meats on medium grind.

4 Grind the pork trimmings and fry. When rendered, use some of the lard to brown the liver, heart and tongue mixture and to cook onions. Stir the mixture as it cooks

5 Add all ingredients in hot state to the rice. Do not allow the lard to get cold and set or it will be harder to get through the sausage stuffer. Add salt and pepper. Mix by hand so as not to smash rice. Taste and add more salt or pepper if needed.

6 Place mixture in stuffer. Pull a length of casing onto the stuffer and fill—not too firm or it will burst when boiling. Tie ends securely with string.

7 Have boiling water in large pot. Place 4 to 5 rings of *hurka* into water bring to boil. As soon as it boils, remove each with wooden spoon carefully so as not to break. Place into a pan of cold water to cool. Repeat until all *hurkas* are done. Set out on counter or table to cook and then refrigerate.

8 Bake in oven until skin is brown or, warm in frying pan, turning over to *hurka* is browned on both sides, 160° inside and crispy outside.

Hungarian Pork Sausage

Kolbász

Often served with hurka *or with* lecsó, kolbász *is very different than Polish kielbasa in the proportions of meats and seasonings.*

5 pounds pork butt, not too lean

1 tablespoon + 1 teaspoon paprika

1 tablespoon + 1 teaspoon salt

1 tablespoon allspice, ground

6 cloves garlic, finely chopped

1 small yellow onion, minced or ground with the pork

1 cup + 2 tablespoons water

1 tablespoon ground fresh black peppercorns

Sausage casing

1 Soak and rinse the casing so it is clean.

2 Grind the pork in a hand grinder or coarsely chop in a food processor.

3 Mix pork with seasoning. If necessary, add water to mixture so it will be soft enough to stuff into the casing. Keep the mixture cold.

4 Check the seasoning: fry a small amount of the mixture and taste it. If it tastes right, add a bit more seasoning because the flavors will mellow over night. If it seems a bit much, it's perfect. Adjust to suit and test again if desired.

5 Refrigerate pork mixture overnight.

6 Place mixture in sausage stuffer and fill casings. Tie ends securely with string.

Tip:

The garlic may be minced and mixed with a bit of water to distribute it more evenly through the pork mixture. Or alternately, boil the garlic for 15 to 20 minutes and mash in a small bit of water to make the slurry. Cool.

See next page for cooking instructions.

In memory of Olga Kish

Hot Hungarian Pork Sausage

Csípős kolbász

Here is an occasion to use hot paprika. Regional and personal preferences determine the mix.

2 pounds
ground pork

1/2 teaspoon
paprika

1/2 teaspoon hot
paprika

1/2 teaspoon ground
caraway seed

1 clove garlic,
chopped fine and
cooked in 1/4 cup
water until mushy

1 small yellow onion,
minced or ground
with the pork

1 cup +
2 tablespoons water

1 tablespoon ground
fresh black pepper-
corns

Adjust seasoning
according to taste

Sausage casing

1 Soak casing in lukewarm water overnight. Next day rinse several times.

2 Mix the pork with the seasonings and regrind the mixture. Keep it cold.

3 Check the seasoning: fry a small amount of the mixture and taste it. If it tastes right, add a bit more seasoning because the flavors will mellow over night. If it seems a bit much, it's perfect. Adjust to suit and test again if desired.

4 Refrigerate overnight.

5 Place mixture in stuffer and stuff into casings. Tie ends securely with string.

Sausages will keep for up to a week to use fresh. They may be frozen.

To fry fresh sausages:

1 Place sausage in a heavy frying pan with a lid. Add about 2 inches of water to the pan, cover, and bring to boil. Reduce heat and simmer. Turn sausages over and add more water if necessary to prevent burning.

2 When both sides have browned, remove lid and continue cooking until no longer pink inside or a thermometer registers 160°.

To roast fresh sausages: Preheat oven to 350° Place sausage in a shallow pan with water in bottom. Roast for 45 minutes until casings become toasty brown, split and until they are no longer pink inside. A meat thermometer should register 160°.

Jerry Takacs

Stewed Peppers & Tomatoes with *Kolbász*

Lecsó és kolbász

Kolbász *provides depth of flavor and completes a meal served with rice.*

5 pounds Hungarian or Romanian yellow peppers

3 large onions

4 medium tomatoes

2 pounds of *kolbász* or turkey kielbasa

2 tablespoons tomato puree

2 -3 teaspoons diced garlic (about 4 cloves)

1 tablespoon paprika

1 teaspoon black pepper

1/2 teaspoon salt

5 tablespoons olive oil

1 Cut the peppers 1-inch x 2-inch strips. Discard veins and seeds. Peel the tomatoes, cut into large pieces. Quarter, then slice the onions. Cut sausage into 1/2-inch pieces..

2 Warm a large skillet and add olive oil. Add onions and cook and stir until translucent. Add diced garlic, cook, stirring for one minute. Remove pan from the heat and stir in paprika.

3 Return pan to heat and add tomatoes, stirring and smoothing with a spoon to create a sauce. Add tomato purée, salt and pepper, peppers and sausage.

4 Cook for 1/2 hour on medium low heat.

Variations

• 2-4 cubes of chicken bouillon may be added in step 3 with the tomato purée.

• This dish may be served with rice.

• Tomatoes may be stewed prior to adding to the skillet.

Serves 6-8

Elizabeth Hunyadi

Kolbász with Lentils

Lencse kolbásszal

A Hungarian version of "franks and beans."

1/2 pound brown lentils

1 pound smoked *kolbász*, 1/4-inch slices or 2-inch pieces

1 cup sour cream

2 tablespoons white vinegar

1 teaspoon salt

1/4 teaspoon dry mustard

1/4 teaspoon sugar

1 quart water

2 tablespoons butter

2 tablespoons flour

1 small red onion, grated

1 teaspoon paprika

1 clove of garlic, crushed

1 cup cold water

1 Wash and clean lentils. In a 4-quart soup pot, boil water. Add lentils and continue boiling for 2 minutes. Set aside, partly covered, for 1 to 1-1/2 hours.

2 Add salt to the water; add *kolbász* and just enough water to cover the ingredients. Bring to a simmer; continue to cook until lentils are tender, approximately 30 minutes.

3 While lentils are cooking, make *rántás*.

4 Add *rántás* to lentils. Add vinegar, mustard, salt, sugar and sour cream and bring to simmer. Simmer for 5 minutes.

Rántás:

Melt butter, add onion and garlic and stir for 1 minute to soften. Add paprika and flour and stir until golden. Stirring, add water until smooth, about 2 minutes.

Serves 6

In memory of Rt. Rev. Dr. Stephen Szabo

Jellied Pigs Feet

Kocsonya

This aspic is considered a delicacy by some and is yet another preparation for pork.

4 whole pigs feet (tails, ears, fresh hocks are optional)

2 cloves garlic, crushed, or more to taste

2 tablespoons salt

1 tablespoon paprika

1 teaspoon whole black peppercorns

1 onion, skin on

About 3 to 3 1/2 quarts water

1 Singe pigs feet over flame (or under broiler), then, scrape and wash thoroughly. Modern butchers may have completed this step for you.

2 Place pigs feet into large pot and add enough cold water to cover. Bring to a boil and skim foam from the top. Add the rest of the ingredients and simmer slowly for about 3 to 4 hours, until the meat separates from the bones.

3 Gently remove meat from the broth and place into soup bowls using a slotted spoon. Let the broth settle for 15 minutes; strain and pour over the meat. Sprinkle with paprika. Cool and place into refrigerator to jell for 24 hours. Serve with rye bread. Can also be sprinkled with vinegar.

Serves 6

In memory of Olga Kish

Fire Roasted Bacon Fry
Sült szalonna

Now a picnic tradition, this fire-roasted bacon is reminiscent of cooking on the Great Plains of Hungary. A Hungarian butcher can supply the szalonna, *which is the specific bacon that makes this so delicious and the aroma so memorable. Good rye bread is a necessity.*

1 loaf Hungarian rye bread or other good rye bread

1 green pepper, diced

1 large onion, diced

2 tomatoes, diced

1 cucumber, diced

1 bunch radishes, diced or sliced thinly

1 pound slab *szalonna* (smoked Hungarian bacon) cut into 4-inch square slabs (about 1/4 pound per person)

Salt and pepper, to taste

1 Make a wood burning fire. Spear the slab of bacon on a campfire skewer or a long and sturdy pointed stick, such as cherry wood. With a sharp knife, make checkerboard slices about 1/4-inch deep into the fat and roast over fire, rotating so fat doesn't drip into fire. When bacon starts to sizzle and fat begins to drip, drizzle the fat onto the bread slices, as much as desired.

2 Place vegetables on the bread slices and season. Add more bacon drippings on top of the vegetables, if desired.

3 When the cracklings are crispy, slice off the slab and sprinkle on the bread with the vegetables. Continue to roast and drizzle the drippings on other bread slices.

Andy Tajgiszer

Stewed Pork Steaks

Sertés szelet

Easy, tasty and for everyone who loves pork.

3 to 4 slices (3/4-inch thick) pork shoulder steak

1 large onion, chopped

1/2 tablespoon paprika

1 clove garlic, minced

Salt, to taste

1 Dredge pork in paprika. Heat a large skillet with a tight-fitting lid and add pork slices. Add onions and sprinkle garlic over pork and add water to cover.

2 Cook, covered on medium heat until cooked through.

3 Remove steaks from pan and place on serving plate. Continue cooking pan juices until reduced for gravy.

In memory of Suzanne Csolty

Fried Pork

Laci pecsenye

Pork and onions demonstrate the "release of flavors" principle of cooking. "Low and slow" is the flavor key. It's easy and so flavorful.

2 pounds pork shoulder steaks

Fat

1 onion, thick sliced

1 teaspoon salt

1/2 teaspoon black pepper, or to taste

1 Melt fat in frying pan. Season pork and fry.

2 Turn meat and add onions. Cover and continue cooking – low and slow – until pork is cooked through.

Serves 4-6

Layered Pork & Rice

Kolozsvári rakottkáposzta

Hungarians love layered sauerkraut dishes. Sour cream tops off the layers.

1 pound pork, cubed

1 tablespoon lard

1 onion, chopped

1 teaspoon paprika

1 teaspoon salt, to taste

1 cup long-grained rice

1 small can sauerkraut, rinsed, drained and squeezed

1/2 cup sour cream

Water, about 1 cup

1 Melt lard; add onion and brown slightly. Add paprika, pork and salt to taste.

2 Brown pork on all sides.

3 Cook rice in boiling, salted water for about 20 minutes. Drain.

4 In a baking dish, arrange a layer of pork mixture; layer of rice and layer of sauerkraut. Continue until all ingredients are used. Pour sour cream over the top. Bake at 350° until browned, about 45 minutes.

Serves 2-4

Violet Sarosi

Pork & Sauerkraut

Székely káposzta

In the 1800's in Budapest, inn patron, Josef Szekely, first ordered this now popular combination of pörkölt and sauerkraut.

2 pound pork, cubed

1 large can
sauerkraut, rinsed
and drained

1/2 cup sour cream

2 tablespoons
shortening or lard

1 onion, chopped

1 tablespoon
paprika

1 clove garlic, minced
or
1 teaspoon
garlic powder

1/2 teaspoon
caraway seed

1 tablespoon flour

Salt and pepper,
to taste

Water, about 1 cup

1 In a large frying pan, cook onions in fat over low heat, stirring frequently. Add pork and brown about 5 minutes. Mix in garlic, caraway, salt and pepper, stirring for about 2 minutes. Pour in water, bring to a simmer and cover.

2 Cook over low heat, about 30 minutes. Add sauerkraut and cook on low heat, about 1 hour, until pork is tender and no longer pink. Add flour, mixing well to thicken. Add sour cream, stirring and heat thoroughly.

Serve with mashed potatoes.

Variation

• Use 1/2 teaspoon paprika; omit garlic and caraway. Omit flour.

Serves 6

Violet Sarosi and in memory of Irene Schnierer

Stuffed Cabbage

Töltött káposzta

"Only stuffed cabbage tastes better reheated"
—old Hungarian saying about this national dish and a duplicitous commentary on life and love.

1 large head green cabbage

1 large onion, chopped

2 tablespoons lard, margarine or oil

1/2 pound ground pork

1/2 pound ground beef

1/3 cup rice

2 teaspoons salt

1 teaspoon paprika

1/2 teaspoon black pepper

2 tablespoons water

1 small can tomato juice or sauce

1 small can sauerkraut

1 clove garlic

1 ham hock or smoked sausage

1 Spear cabbage head with a fork and place in a large pot of boiling water. With a knife, cut away leaves as they wilt, removing from water. When all leaves are removed, cut away the thick vein on the back of the leaf.

2 Cook and stir onion in fat until golden; set aside to cool.

3 In a bowl, mix meats, rice, seasonings, onion and water.

4 To stuff the leaves, place a leaf in your left hand. Place a tablespoon of meat mixture into the leaf. With the right hand, fold one side of the leaf over the meat and roll up. Tuck the loose end into the roll firmly but gently.

5 In a large pot, place the meat on the bottom and cover it with chopped cabbage and some of the sauerkraut. Add the cabbage rolls in layers. Follow with the rest of the chopped cabbage and sauerkraut. Pour the tomato sauce over the layers and enough water to cover. Add clove of garlic if desired.

6 Cook over a low flame for 1-1/2 to 2 hours until rice is cooked through.

In memory of Olga Kish

74

Stuffed Kohlrabi

Töltött karalábé

Stuffed vegetables are common in Hungarian cooking. Kohlrabi, very popular in Hungary, is rumored to have been brought by Attila the Hun.

6 new young kohlrabi, peeled and center hollowed to form a 1/4-inch shell, pulp, chopped and reserved

1 small onion, chopped fine

1/2 cup cooked rice

1 pound ground pork or
1/2 pound ground pork and 1/2 pound ground veal

2 cloves garlic, minced

1/2 teaspoon paprika

1/4 teaspoon pepper

2 tablespoons chopped fresh parsley, divided

1 egg

1 teaspoon dried marjoram or 1-2 tablespoons chopped fresh

Salt to taste

3 tablespoons butter

3 tablespoons flour

1 In a 1 quart saucepan, bring salted water to a boil and add kohlrabi, bring to a simmer and cook until tender, about 10 minutes Drain.

2 In a small frying pan, heat fat and add onions, garlic and kohlrabi pulp. Cook, stirring, until onions are translucent, about 5 minutes. Cool.

3 In a mixing bowl, combine onion mixture with meat and seasonings and fill kohlrabies, mounding slightly over the tops.

4 Place kohlrabies in covered baking dish or saucepan with stock or water with 1 teaspoon salt and 1/2 teaspoon pepper to come half way up the sides of the kohlrabies. Bring liquid to a boil, reduce heat, cover and simmer 35 to 45 minutes until meat is cooked through.

5 Reserving pan juices, remove kohlrabi from pan and place on serving dish. Melt butter in a small saucepan and stir in flour, browning slightly. Whisk in 1 cup of the reserved pan juices, adding water if less than 1 cup. Stir until thickened. Pour over kohlrabi and sprinkle with 1 tablespoon freshly chopped parsley or marjoram.

Serves 6 as a side dish

Mark Shary

Stuffed Peppers/Creamy sauce

Töltött paprika

The Hungarian passion for peppers is demonstrated again in this classic. These two excellent recipes showcase two styles of sauce.

1/2 pound ground beef

1/2 pound ground pork

1/2 cup rice, washed and uncooked

1 egg

1 medium onion, minced

1-1/2 teaspoon salt

1/2 teaspoon pepper

1 teaspoon paprika

6 to 8 medium green peppers

3 to 4 cups tomato juice

1 cup water

3 tablespoons shortening

Rántas

1 tablespoon flour

1 tablespoon shortening

2 tablespoons milk

1 small onion, minced

1 cup sour cream

1 Cut tops off peppers, remove core and seeds and discard. Rinse peppers inside and out.

2 In a small frying pan, brown onions in shortening, stirring constantly. Cool to room temperature.

3 In a large bowl, mix all ingredients, except tomato juice. Add cooled onions.

4 Loosely stuff mixture into peppers filling to 1/4 inch from top of each pepper.

5 Place peppers in deep pot. If any meat remains, shape into balls and add to pot. Cover with tomato juice. Add water. Bring to a boil, reduce to simmer then cover and cook for 1-1/2 to 2 hours. To prevent sticking, shake pot occasionally.

Rántás

1 In a small frying pan, heat shortening and add onions, cooking until translucent. Stir in flour and brown slightly, stirring constantly.

2 Add milk, stirring and bring to a boil. Add sour cream. Slowly add some of the tomato juice from the peppers. Pour over stuffed peppers and return to a boil.

Serves 3-4

Elaine Galgany

Stuffed Peppers/Chunky sauce

Töltött paprika

As an alternative in either recipe, use sweet red peppers or substitute ground turkey.

1 pound
ground beef

1/4 pound
ground pork

1/2 cup rice

1 small onion, minced

1/2 teaspoon salt

1/4 teaspoon pepper

6 to 8 medium
green peppers

1-1/2 cup chopped
tomatoes or small can
tomatoes

1 cup water

3 tablespoons
shortening

1 tablespoon flour

2 tablespoons
water

1 cup sour cream

1 to 2 tablespoons
sugar, to taste

1 Cook rice about 15 minutes, until almost done and cool.

2 Cook and strain fresh tomatoes or cook canned tomatoes about 15 minutes.

3 Mix 1 tablespoon flour with 2 tablespoons water until smooth. Add sour cream. Slowly stir this mixture into the cooked tomatoes over low heat, stirring constantly. Add sugar and cook a few minutes. Set aside.

4 Cut off tops of peppers, remove core and seeds; discard.

5 In a large bowl, mix ground meats, cooled rice, onion, salt and pepper.

6 Loosely stuff mixture into peppers filling to 1/2 inch from top of each pepper.

7 Place in a deep pot or kettle with enough water to cover. Simmer, covered over low heat about 1 hour until meat is cooked. Gently lift the peppers into the tomato sauce and cook about 15 minutes. Serve hot with *nokedli*.

Variation

• Use 1-1/4 pound ground turkey instead of beef and pork.

Serves 3-4

Veal Paprikas

Borjú paprikas

This "elegant" beef stew pairs nicely with a cucumber or green salad and good bread to soak up the sauce.

1 pound veal, cut into large cubes

1 tablespoon oil or spray pan

1 small onion

1 teaspoon paprika

1 teaspoon flour

1/2 cup sour cream

Salt and pepper, to taste

1 In a large frying pan, cook the onion in the oil until translucent. Add the veal and brown the cubes on all side over medium high heat.

2 Remove from heat and stir in paprika, salt and pepper. Add enough water or stock to barely cover the meat. Cover, return to low heat and simmer slowly until tender, about an hour.

3 Mix the flour into the sour cream and add some of the juices from the pan into the sour cream to temper it. Whisk the sour cream into the pan and stir constantly to mix and develop the flavors, about 5 to 10 minutes.

Serve with broad noodles or small dumplings.

Serves 4

Julianna Kovach Zingale

78

Veal Hortobagy

Hortobagy palacsinta

Savory pancakes may be served as appetizers or an entrée.

Palacsinta

2 cups milk

2 eggs

1-1/2 cups flour

1/4 teaspoon salt

Veal Filling

1 pound veal, cut into very small cubes

1 tablespoon oil

1 small onion

1 teaspoon paprika

1 teaspoon flour

1 cup sour cream

Salt and pepper, to taste

1 In a medium bowl, beat eggs, Add milk, then gradually add flour and salt. Beat until smooth. If batter is thick, add a bit more milk to bring to the consistency of a pourable thin batter.

2 Heat a medium skillet very hot. Lightly grease or spray with oil for the first pancake only. A non-stick frying pan works equally well. Pour a scant 1/4 cup of batter into the pan and rotate to spread over the entire bottom of the pan. Flip pancake when set and lacy brown and brown the opposite side. Remove to plate. Cook remaining batter. Set aside.

3 In a large frying pan, cook the onion in the oil until translucent. Add the veal and brown over medium high heat, stirring constantly.

4 Remove from heat and stir in paprika, salt and pepper. Add enough water to prevent the meat from scorching. Cover, place pan on low heat and simmer until tender. Remove meat; set aside.

Preheat oven to 350°

5 Mix the flour into the sour cream and add some of the juices from the pan into the sour cream to temper it. Whisk the sour cream into the pan and bring to a boil, stirring constantly to mix and develop the flavors. Add some of the sauce to the meat and fill pancake. Roll up.

6 Place rolled pancakes in a baking dish and pour remaining sauce over the top. Place in oven and heat through.

Palacsinta in memory of Olga Kish

79

Veal Slices Hungarian Style

Rántott borjúhús

The veal reveals its flavor with a spritz of lemon upon serving. Preparation is quick once the meat is breaded.

4 6-ounce veal slices

4 tablespoons (1/2 stick) butter, melted

1-1/2 cups bread crumbs (4 ounces)

1/2 cup grated Parmesan cheese, optional

1 teaspoon salt

1 tablespoon black pepper

2 eggs, lightly beaten

Oil to fry

1 Pound both sides of veal. Score the surface of the meat, but do not cut through. Salt veal slices.

2 Melt butter in a small saucepan and cool slightly. Pour into a plate or shallow bowl large enough for veal slices. In another shallow bowl, mix grated cheese, if using, with bread crumbs and pepper.

3 Dip veal into butter to coat both sides. Dredge in bread crumbs. Then dip it into egg, and dredge in bread crumbs again.

4 Heat oil to medium hot and fry on both sides for 3 minutes, until golden brown.

Variations

• Chicken or pork may be substituted for the veal.

• 1 tablespoon fresh minced garlic may be added to the bread crumbs.

Serves 4

Andrea and Albert Ladanyi

Veal & Paprikas Potatoes

Borjúhúsos paprikás krumpli

This easy one-pan meal is a short-cut preparation, but long on flavor.

4 veal chops

1 tablespoon oil

1 large onion, sliced

3 to 4 potatoes, cubed

3 cloves garlic, sliced

Salt and pepper, to taste

1 teaspoon paprika

1 can tomato soup + 1 can water

1 In a large non-stick frying pan, heat oil over medium heat. Add veal chops and brown both sides. Remove chops from pan and set aside.

2 Add onion, potatoes, garlic and seasonings to pan. Brown. Return chops to pan.

3 Pour soup and water over the chops, cover and simmer over low heat, about 1 hour until potatoes are tender and veal is cooked through.

Serves 4

Melissa Bibbo

Cabbage Noodles – *Káposztás tészta*, page 86

NOODLES & DUMPLINGS

Csiga Noodles, page 84

NOODLES AND DUMPLINGS MAY BE SERVED AS A MAIN COURSE, AS AN ACCOMPANIMENT TO SOUP OR AS DESSERT. VARIOUS SHAPES ARE SPECIFIC TO CERTAIN DISHES. *TÉSZTA* (HOMEMADE NOODLES) ARE CUT INTO LARGE OR SMALL SQUARES OR SLICED INTO RIBBONS. SMALL SQUARES ROLLED ON A GROOVED WOODEN BOARD WITH A POINTED STICK FORM *CSIGA*, USED IN SOUPS. *TARHONYA* (PASTA PELLETS) ARE MADE WITH A BOX GRATER AND DRIED, TO BE RECONSTITUTED AND USED IN SOUPS AND STEWS OR BROWNED AND SEASONED LIKE PILAF. *CSIPETKE* ARE PINCHED NOODLES. *GALUSKA* (DUMPLINGS) ARE SOFT, WHILE *NOKEDLI* (DROP NOODLES) ARE FIRM, BUT BOTH ARE SERVED IN STEWS AND SOUPS. FRUIT-FILLED *GOMBOC* DUMPLINGS MAY BE SERVED AS A SAVORY ENTRÉE OR TRANSFORMED INTO A DELICIOUS DESSERT TOPPED WITH A SPRINKLING OF NUTS OR A DUSTING OF SPARKLING WHITE SUGAR.

Homemade Noodles

Házi tészta

*This is the church's Noodle Makers' recipe.
Traditional serving ways follow.*

2-1/2 pounds flour
(unbleached
all purpose)

6 eggs

1 cup water, about

1 Place flour into the bowl of a five-quart electric mixer fitted with the dough hook. Start mixer and add eggs. Slowly add water in a steady stream and mix until dough forms and gathers together into a stiff dough. Turn onto a lightly floured surface and knead until smooth. Let dough rest 30 minutes, covered with slightly damp towel. This allows glutens in flour to relax and lengthen.

2 Cut dough into 4 pieces. Roll a single piece medium thin, either on a lightly floured board with a rolling pin or through a hand pasta machine set at the second to last setting so that the dough is about the thickness of a penny. Let rest on a dry towel until slightly dry, but still pliable, approximately 30 minutes.

3 Fold dough in fourths, like a handkerchief and cut with a very sharp knife into half-inch strips or one-inch squares. Separate dough and let dry completely, uncovered on dry towels. Fans may speed the process and prevent mold.

4 Store in plastic bags or glass containers.

To cook noodles:

1 Bring a large stock pot of water to a boil and add 1 teaspoon of salt.

2 Cook noodles for about 5 minutes or until soft.

3 Drain. Serve with soups, meat dishes, or mix with any of the following ingredients.

Marge Jacob

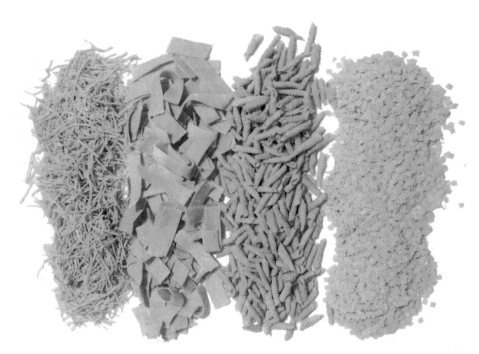

To noodles, add the following, adjusting to taste:

Walnuts
Dio

Grind walnuts and brown in a skillet with a little butter. Mix with sugar to taste. Add to noodles.

Poppy Seed
Mák

Mix poppy seed with sugar to taste. Add a small amount of milk and cook about 10 minutes and toss with noodles.

Cheese
Túró

Mix dry or drained cottage cheese or dry or drained cottage cheese with half as much cream cheese or sour cream and then toss with warmed buttered noodles. Serve, sprinkled with white sugar or crumbled cooked bacon, if desired.

Farina
Gríz

Fry 14 ounces farina in butter, until brown. Add 2 teaspoons salt and 4 cups of water and cover. Cook until soft. Mix with the noodles. Add additional salt or sugar to taste.

Apricot
Sárgabarack

Add sugar to taste to 1 cup *lekvar* and mix with noodles.

Other recipes follow >

85

Cabbage & Noodles

Káposztás tészta

Enjoyed anytime, this comfort food is paired with pork roast on New Year's Day for good luck.

Wide noodles, cooked (about 10 to 12 ounces, dry)

1/4 pound (1 stick) butter or margarine, melted

2 medium heads of green cabbage

1 teaspoon salt

1 small onion

1 tablespoon butter or margarine

1 Chop, grate or use food processor to chop cabbage until medium fine. Sprinkle with salt and let stand 10 minutes. Squeeze out liquid. In a large heavy skillet, melt the butter or margarine and add the chopped cabbage. Cook over low heat, stirring often with a wooden spoon until lightly browned and tender.

2 Cook chopped onion in butter or margarine, stirring constantly until lightly golden brown. Add to cabbage. Combine with the cooked noodles.

Variations

- Fry cabbage in 1/4 pound butter and 1/2 cup bacon fat slowly for 40 minutes. Proceed as above. Or, use less bacon fat and butter, as desired.

- Cabbage may be covered and steamed a bit before adding noodles.

- A teaspoon of sugar may be added to the cabbage to caramelize it a bit.

Irene Kita and Brenda Rohaly

Grated Noodles

Reszelt tészta

Nomadic Magyars invented and packed this noodle as they traversed the Great Hungarian Plain. Dried in the sun, it kept indefinitely for their travels.

1 egg, slightly beaten

1 cup flour

1/4 teaspoon salt

1 In a bowl mix flour and salt with egg. Knead into a hard ball.

2 Grate on the round holes of a potato grater or chop fine with a large chef's knife to the size of small peas. Spread out on a towel to dry.

3 Cook in boiling water until tender or make *tarhonya* described below. Serve with stew or as a side dish.

Toasted Browned Noodles

Tarhonya

This procedure, much like pilaf brought by the Turks, reconstitutes the hard dried noodles.

1 pound grated noodles (above)

2 tablespoons lard, butter or margarine

1 tablespoon minced onion

1/2 to 1 teaspoon salt

1/4 teaspoon pepper

1/4 teaspoon paprika, optional

About 1 quart water or soup stock

1 In a skillet or 4 quart saucepan, fry noodles in fat until golden brown, stirring frequently; add onions and cook a few minutes longer. Add salt, pepper and paprika if using and enough water or soup stock to cover the noodles.

2 Cook about 20 minutes; if noodles are still hard, add more liquid and continue cooking until noodles are soft. Adjust seasoning to taste. Serve with *paprikás, pörkölt, tokány* or roasted meats or poultry.

In memory of Olga Kish

Cheese or Lekvar Filled Dumplings
Derelye

Usually a dessert, these filled dumplings are a satisfying meal. Savory fillings may also be used.

3 cups flour

3 eggs

1/4 cup water

1/4 pound (1 stick) butter

1 cup bread crumbs

1 pound lekvar

Cottage cheese filling, below

Boiling water + 1 teaspoon salt

Cheese Filling:

1 pound dry cottage cheese

1 egg yolk

Dash of salt

Sugar, to taste, about 2 to 4 tablespoons

1 In a small skillet, melt butter and toast bread crumbs. Remove from heat and cool.

2 In a large bowl, beat eggs and water. Add flour and knead into a firm ball. Let the dough stand 20 minutes, covered with the inverted bowl.

3 Knead again until smooth. Let dough rest 10 minutes, covered with the inverted bowl. Bring pot of water to boil, add salt and simmer until ready to use.

4 Roll dough on pastry board until 1/8-inch thick. Cut into 2-inch squares and fill half of the squares with 1 teaspoon of cheese or *lekvar* filling; fold over to form a triangle and press edges tightly to seal. Dough that is too thin or not tightly sealed will break apart while boiling

5 Drop dumplings into boiling water and cook until noodles rise to top, about 5 minutes. Drain and rinse in cold water. Lightly butter noodles and toss with the bread crumbs.

Cheese Filling:

Mash cottage cheese or put through a sieve. Mix in egg yolk, salt and sugar to taste.

Plum Dumplings

Szilvásgombóc

*The addition of potato to the dough adds body.
Fresh Italian plums in the center are a sweet delight.*

4 medium
Idaho potatoes,
peeled and cubed

2 to 3 cups flour

1/2 teaspoon salt

1 egg

1/4 pound (1 stick)
butter or margarine

1 cup bread crumbs

2 teaspoons sugar

1 pound small fresh
Italian plums, pitted
and cut in halves and
mixed with enough
cinnamon-sugar to
sweeten, depending
on plums

1 Cook potatoes in boiling water until tender.
Drain, mash and cool.

2 Mix potatoes, eggs, salt and flour and knead
on a floured board to a firm dough.

3 Roll to 1/2-inch thick and cut into 2 x 2-inch
squares. Place about 1/2 teaspoon of filling in
each square. Pinch to close and make shape into
small balls.

4 Drop dumplings into pot of boiling water and
cook 10 minutes. Remove with slotted spoon
and place in serving dish.

5 Melt butter or margarine and brown bread
crumbs. Toss with dumplings and sugar.

Variation

• Instead of plum filling, soften 1 pound prunes
in warm water, drain and purée. Use 1/2 to 1
teaspoon for filling.

Helen Gyerman – in memory of her mother

Drop Dumplings

Nokedli

Two basic recipes for drop dumplings, soft or firm.

3 eggs, beaten

3 cups flour

3 tablespoons sour cream

1 teaspoon salt

1/2 cup water

1 Place flour and salt in a mixing bowl or on a board and make a well at the center. Add eggs, water and sour cream. Mix all ingredients and beat with a spoon, fork or whisk.

2 Drop batter by teaspoonfuls into salted boiling water. Cook about 10 minutes until dumplings float to the top and are cooked through. Drain and rinse with cold water. Add to *paprikás*, stew or brown in butter.

Variation

• For a extra firm dumpling, use 1-1/2 cup flour, adding more if necessary to make a stiff batter. Drop batter from tip of spoon or tip of knife into boiling water. Cook 8 to 10 minutes. Rinse in cold water and drain.

Anne Sabo

Cheese-filled Dumplings
Túrós derelye

A sweet noodle dish may be served several times a week in a Hungarian home.

1 pound
dry cottage cheese

1 cup flour

1 tablespoon farina

4 eggs

1 teaspoon salt

1/4 pound (1 stick)
butter

1/4 cup toasted bread
crumbs

1 Put cottage cheese through a ricer or strainer.

2 In a large bowl, beat eggs and salt. Add cheese, flour and farina and mix thoroughly.

3 Roll teaspoonfuls of dough with a little flour and roll into a ball. Place cheese balls on a tray Drop into boiling salted water and cook 15 to 20 minutes. Remove dumplings with slotted spoon and place in serving dish.

4 In separate pan, melt butter and add dumplings. Add toasted bread crumbs and gently mix.

Variations

- Sprinkle finished dumplings with confectioner's sugar and serve with sour cream.

- Pot cheese or farmer's cheese (not the slicing kind) may be substituted for dry cottage cheese.

Farina Dumplings #1

Grízgombóc

Farina adds "bite" and the eggs make them light!

3 eggs
1/2 teaspoon salt
3/4 cup farina

1 Whip eggs in small bowl with 1/2 teaspoon salt. Slowly mix in farina until smooth and creamy. Let stand for about 30 minutes.

2 Working quickly, drop small bits of dough from the tip of a spoon into soup or boiling water; cook until tender, about 20 minutes.

In memory of Elsie Skomski – her mother's recipe

Farina Dumplings #2

Grízgombóc

Half flour and half farina lightens the "bite."

1/2 cup flour
1/2 cup farina
1/2 teaspoon salt
1 egg beaten with 1 teaspoon water
1 to 3 tablespoons water, as needed

Bring a pan of water to a boil while making dough.

1 Sift dry ingredients together. Make a well in center and add beaten egg-water, incorporating with fork or whisk. Gradually add additional water and beat about 4 minutes until the dough is stiff and shiny.

2 Working quickly, cut small bits of the dough – about 1/4 teaspoon – from the tip of a spoon into boiling water and boil about 15 to 20 minutes until center is cooked through. Drain.

In memory of Ethel Kovach

Liver Dumplings

Máj galuska

An example of a savory dumpling.

6 chicken livers or 1/2 pound calves liver, ground or chopped

1/2 teaspoon salt

2 eggs, lightly beaten

1/2 teaspoon grated onion

1-1/4 cup flour

2 teaspoons chopped parsley

2 tablespoons water

2 tablespoons fine bread crumbs

1 Place liver in bowl. Add salt, parsley, eggs and water. Blend gently. Add flour and bread crumbs and mix to make a soft dough.

2 Drop from tip of knife or spoon into boiling, salted water. Cook 5 minutes.

3 Drain in colander and rinse in cold water. Serve in hot chicken soup.

In memory of Olga Kish

Parsley Dumplings

Petrezselymes nokedli

It's the baking powder that makes these a fluffy dumpling. The parsley imparts a herbal flavor and a touch of color.

1-1/2 cups flour

2 teaspoons baking powder

1/2 teaspoons salt

1 tablespoon margarine

3/4 cup milk

1 egg, beaten

1-1/2 tablespoons finely chopped parsley

1 Sift flour, baking powder and salt twice. Cut in margarine with fork or pastry cutter. Make a well in flour mixture, stir in milk, egg and parsley with a fork, incorporating flour until it forms into a sticky dough.

2 Drop by teaspoon into salted, boiling water. Cook about 10 minutes, until cooked through. Rinse the dumplings in colander with cold water, drain and serve with paprikas or stew.

Betty Hartman

Grated Potato Dumplings

Reszelt krumly nokedli

Serve hot with sour cream, cottage cheese or cream cheese or pair with sauerkraut or sautéed sweet cabbage. Delicious browned with onions and paprika.

3 medium Idaho potatoes, peeled

1 teaspoon salt

1 egg

1 cup flour, or more

1 tablespoon salt for boiling water

4 tablespoons (1/2 stick) butter

1 Grate potatoes into large bowl. Add 1 teaspoon of salt, egg and flour to make stiff dough.

2 Bring a large pot of water to a boil and add salt. Cut potato batter into water from tip of spoon or knife to form dumplings. Cook until dumplings rise to the top, at least 5 to 8 minutes. Drain in colander and rinse with cold water.

3 In a large pot, melt butter, add dumplings and serve with one of the options above.

In memory of Olga Kish

Cooked Potato Dumplings

Angyalbögyörő

Every culture has its version of potato dumplings, and with good reason: mmmmm.

4 medium Idaho
potatoes

2 to 3 cups flour

1 teaspoon salt

1 egg, beaten

1/4 pound (1 stick)
butter

1 cup bread crumbs

2 tablespoons sugar

Salt and pepper to
taste, optional

1 Cook potatoes in a 4 quart pan with water to cover until soft; drain. Shake pan of potatoes over the flame until they are dry. Cool to touch, peel. Put potatoes through ricer and cool.

2 In a large bowl, mix riced potatoes, salt, egg, flour and knead until dough is not sticky and fairly firm. Roll pieces of dough into long ropes, the thickness of a finger. Cut into 1-inch pieces. Place on a tray. Bring a large pot of water to a simmer. Working in batches, drop dumplings into simmering water.

3 Cook 5 to 8 minutes. Remove and drain. Repeat with remaining dumplings.

4 Melt butter in a skillet; add bread crumbs and brown lightly; mix in dumplings and heat through.

5 Salt to taste. Serve warm, sprinkled with sugar, if desired.

In memory of Olga Kish

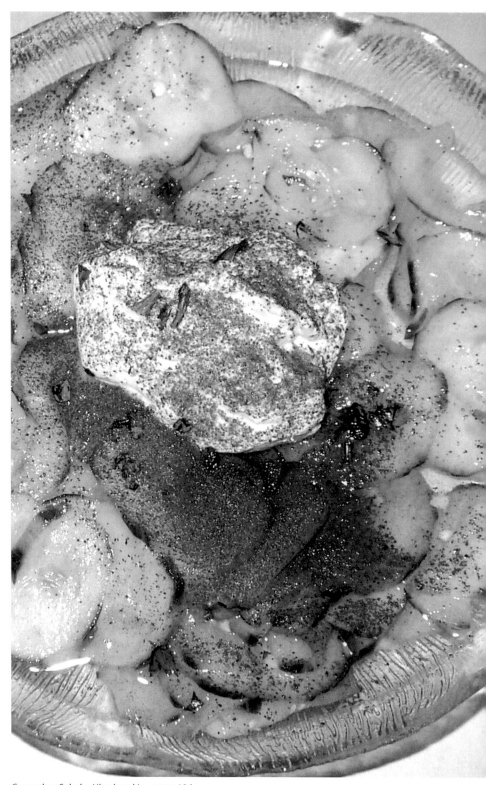

Cucumber Salad – *Uborkasaláta*, page 106

VEGETABLES & SALADS

Pickles – *Uborka*, page 108

VEGETABLES COME TO THE TABLE DRESSED! AS SIDE DISHES, THEY ARE BRAISED, THICKENED, CREAMED OR STUFFED AND OFTEN SEASONED TO CONTRAST WITH AND COMPLEMENT THE RICH ENTRÉES WITH WHICH THEY ARE SERVED. SALADS ARE SIMPLE: CRISP LETTUCE, CUCUMBERS, GARDEN-FRESH TOMATOES, PEPPERS, ONIONS AND CABBAGE, INDIVIDUALLY OR IN COMBINATION, ARE ACCENTED WITH A SLIGHTLY TART-SWEET MIX OF VINEGAR, WATER, SALT AND SUGAR TO BRIGHTEN AND REFRESH THE PALATE. GARDEN-KEEPING IS A TIME-HONORED HUNGARIAN TRADITION, BOTH FOR THE FRESH HARVEST IT SUPPLIES AND AS A WAY OF SERVING THE ONE WHO PROVIDES.

Pickled Beets

Céklasaláta

Summer beets in abundance can be preserved to be enjoyed all year.

7 pounds beets, scrubbed, beet tops removed

4 cups sugar

4 cups water

4 cups white vinegar

1 In a large pot, cover beets with cold water, bring to a simmer and cook beets until fork tender, depending on size of beets. Drain, cool and peel.

2 Chunk or slice beets into sterile pint jars.

3 In a large noncorrosive pot, add sugar, water and vinegar. Heat to boil. Remove from heat. Pour liquid over beets. Cool to room temperature. Cover with jar lids.

Makes 6-8 pints.

Ann Kovach

Beet Greens; Spinach or Swiss Chard

Cékla zöldség

"Don't throw those beet tops out!"
—Mom.

1 pound beet greens

2 quarts water

1 teaspoon salt

Butter, to taste

White or red wine vinegar, to taste

1 In a saucepan, bring water to a boil and salt. Add greens and cook briefly until tender. Drain liquid and discard. Place butter on warm greens until melted and stir to coat.

2 Sprinkle with vinegar to taste.

Variation

• Swiss chard and spinach may be used with or in place of the beet greens.

Beets and Horseradish

Tormás cékla

The versatile beet, used here in a fresh salad, is dressed with added zing from horseradish.

2 pounds whole beets, cooked and peeled

1 4-oz jar prepared white horseradish

2 tablespoons white vinegar

1 tablespoon sugar

1 Grate beets into a large bowl.

2 Add horseradish, vinegar and sugar. Mix well.

3 Refrigerate.

Richard Sarosi

Fresh Horseradish

Ecetes torma mártás

Horseradish grows easily in backyard gardens and is readily available in farmer's markets. Brace yourself for the strong aroma when grating.

1 horseradish root, about 16 oz

1-1/2 teaspoons white or cider vinegar

1/2 teaspoon salt

1 teaspoon sugar

1 Peel and grate horseradish into a small bowl.

2 Add vinegar, salt and sugar. Mix well.

3 Refrigerate.

Variation

• 2 tablespoons sour cream may be added.

Gizella Dienes

Black, White & Red Radish Salad
Reteksaláta

Peppery hot, this salad adds zing when used as a condiment served with salted or smoked meats.

1 small black radish

5 white icicle radishes

15 red radishes

1/2 cup white wine vinegar

1 teaspoon toasted mustard seeds

1 teaspoon salt

2 teaspoons sugar

1 Scrub and trim all the radishes. To mellow the heat and bitterness of the black radishes, peel, slice thin and cover with cold water. Place in refrigerator overnight or up to three days. Drain. Rinse, drain again and pat dry.

2 Thinly slice red radishes and icicle radishes. Mix with black radish.

3 Mix vinegar, salt, sugar and mustard seeds. Toss with radishes.

Mark Shary

Green Beans with Vinegar
Ecetes zöldbab

The sauce should not be too thick, just enough to envelop the beans.

3/4 pound green beans, ends trimmed.

2 tablespoons butter or oil

1 to 2 tablespoons flour

1/2 cup sliced onion

1/4 cup white or red wine vinegar

1 to 2 teaspoons sugar, to taste

1 In a saucepan, bring water to a boil and simmer beans until tender. Drain and set aside.

2 In a small frying pan, heat butter or oil then add onions and cook, stirring, until translucent. Blend in flour and continue stirring, to brown.

3 Add up to 1 cup of water, sugar and vinegar then stir while sauce thickens. Add beans to coat.

Variations

• Add 1/2 teaspoon of paprika to onions.

• Add snipped fresh dill to taste.

Cabbage with Tomatoes

Paradicsomos káposzta

Classic Eastern European fare.

1 medium head green cabbage, outer leaves removed and discarded

6 to 8 tomatoes, ripe

1 onion, chopped

1 cup sour cream

2 cups water

1/4 cup flour

Salt, pepper and sugar, to taste

3 tablespoons butter

1 Cut cabbage into small wedges, set aside.

2 Blanche and peel tomatoes, chop.

3 Place cabbage and tomatoes into a soup pot and add water, salt and pepper. Simmer about 20 to 25 minutes until cabbage is soft.

4 In a small bowl, mix sour cream with flour until smooth, add some water from cabbage/tomato mixture and stir well. Gradually add to cabbage, stirring constantly. Simmer 5 minutes longer.

5 In a small saucepan, cook onion in butter, stirring until golden. Add to cabbage and mix well.

In memory of Mary Kovach

Sweet & Sour Red Cabbage
Dinsztelt Káposzta

Bacon fat marries with the onion to provide the depth of flavor to this colorful classic.

1 head of red cabbage (about 2 pounds)

4 tablespoons bacon fat

1 medium onion

3 cloves garlic

1 cup water

1/3 cup vinegar

1/2 teaspoon salt

1 Cut the cabbage into four sections and slice thinly.

2 In a large skillet, melt the bacon drippings. Mince the onion and garlic, add to the skillet and cook, stirring until softened. Add water, vinegar and salt. Add the cabbage and continue cooking on low heat, stirring frequently so the cabbage doesn't burn. Cover. Cook for 30 to 45 minutes until cabbage is soft.

Serves 6-8

Elaine Galgany

Vinegar Cabbage Slaw
Ecetes káposztasaláta

A heavily-sauced meat dish or fish pair perfectly with this healthful salad.

1/2 head cabbage, sliced very thin

1/4 onion

1/8 green pepper

1/4 cup white vinegar

1/4 cup water

1-1/2 tablespoons sugar

2 teaspoons salt

1/4 teaspoon pepper

1 Salt the cabbage and chill at least 30 minutes. Squeeze out liquid. Slice the onion very thin and thinly chop the green pepper, if using. Place in bowl with cabbage.

2 Mix the dressing thoroughly and toss with cabbage mixture. Chill until serving.

Variation

• Add 1/8 teaspoon celery seed.

Serves 6

In memory of Ethel Kovach

Red & Green Cabbage with Caraway

Köménymagos káposzta

Colorful, aromatic, spicy, sweet and sour, these flavors sing of Hungarian tradition.

1/2 head of red cabbage, cut fine

1/2 head green cabbage, cut fine

2 quarts boiling water

1-1/2 tablespoon shortening

3 to 4 whole cloves

1/4 teaspoon caraway seeds

Salt and pepper, to taste

1/4 cup vinegar

1/4 cup sugar

1 Place red cabbage in colander and pour boiling water over to soften. Let drain.

2 In a dutch oven or noncorrosive pot, melt shortening and add green cabbage. Cook over medium low heat, stirring frequently until softened and lightly golden. Add red cabbage, stir.

3 Add cloves and caraway seeds, stir. Cover and reduce heat to low and cook about 5 minutes more, or until cabbage is tender. Season with salt and pepper.

4 Mix vinegar and sugar in a small cup until sugar is dissolved. Pour over cabbage mixture and heat thoroughly.

Variation

• 4 Granny Smith apples, peeled, cored and sliced thinly may be added during the cooking of the green cabbage to sweeten.

Serves 8

Spiced Carrots

Fűszerezett sárgarépa

The spicy accents to these carrots are a satisfying and fragrant autumn/wintertime treat.

4 to 6 carrots

1 teaspoon salt

1 tablespoon white vinegar

2 tablespoons honey, brown sugar or white sugar

4 tablespoons (1/2 stick) butter, melted

1/8 teaspoon each nutmeg and cinnamon

2 to 3 whole cloves

1 Peel and slice carrots into 1/8-inch medallions. In a covered saucepan, simmer carrots in salted water until tender. Drain.

2 Combine vinegar with honey, brown sugar or white sugar. Add butter, cloves, nutmeg and cinnamon. Pour over carrots. Reheat.

Serves 6

Buttered Carrots with Herbs

Sárgarépa vajjal

Simple buttered carrots easily absorb the Hungarian essential flavors.

4 to 6 carrots, peeled and sliced into rounds

1 teaspoon salt

2 tablespoons butter

1 tablespoon fresh parsley or dill or 1 teaspoon dried tarragon

1 teaspoon sugar

1 In a medium saucepan, bring water to boil; add salt and carrots, simmering until barely tender, about 7 minutes. Drain.

2 In the same pan, melt butter over low heat and add parsley, dill or tarragon and sugar. Cook and stir for 1 minute, add carrots and heat through.

Serves 6

Cauliflower with Sour Cream
Tejfeles karfiol

Transform cauliflower into an elegant side dish with this flavorful, easy-to-assemble casserole.

1 medium head cauliflower, cleaned and broken into flowerets

1 cup sour cream

1/2 cup milk

1/2 cup unseasoned bread crumbs

3 tablespoons butter

1/2 teaspoon salt

1 Boil salted water and cook cauliflower until tender but still firm, about 5 minutes. Drain.

2 Mix sour cream and milk. Dip cauliflowerettes into the sour cream mixture and then into bread crumbs. Place in buttered baking dish and top with extra crumbs. Dot with sour cream.

3 Bake 30 minutes at 350°. Sprinkle with paprika to garnish.

Serves 6

Elaine Galgany

Cauliflower with Creamy Saffron Sauce
Karfiol sáfrányszósszal

Warm, colorful and easy to prepare, this is a beautiful accompaniment to chicken or pork.

1 medium head cauliflower, broken into flowerets

1 pinch saffron

1/4 teaspoon paprika

3 tablespoons butter

3 tablespoons flour

Paprika for garnish

Salt and pepper, to taste

1 Bring enough water to cover cauliflower to a boil with saffron, paprika and salt. Add cauliflower and simmer 10 minutes or until tender. Drain, reserving 2 cups liquid.

2 In a saucepan, make a sauce by melting butter and adding flour stirring constantly until golden. Gradually whisk in reserved liquid and simmer until thickened slightly. Toss cauliflower to coat and sprinkle with paprika.

Serves 6

Cucumber Salad
Uborkasaláta

A cooling salad with a slightly sweet bite. Step 1 ensures cucumbers will not be bitter.

2 medium cucumbers

1-1/2 teaspoon salt

3 tablespoons white vinegar

3 tablespoons water

1/2 teaspoon sugar

1 small onion, thinly sliced

1/8 teaspoon black pepper, or to taste

Paprika

1 Peel and thinly slice cucumbers. Sprinkle with salt and toss. Let stand 30 minutes; squeeze slices discarding liquid and place in serving bowl.

2 Mix remaining ingredients; pour over cucumbers and mix gently. Sprinkle with sweet paprika. Chill 1 to 2 hours. Garnish with sprinkle of paprika.

Serves 6

Betty Rose Galgany

Cucumbers with Sour Cream
Tejfeles Uborkasaláta

The addition of sour cream makes a totally different dish in both appearance and taste. It's creaminess complements any roast.

Recipe above

1/2 to 1 cup sour cream, to taste

Follow the recipe above and gently stir sour cream into the dressing before chilling.

Serves 6

Irene Kita; Betty Rose Galgany

"Cooked" Cucumber Salad

Uborkasaláta

Preparation in this manner makes the cucumbers easily digestible.

2 large cucumbers, peeled

Boiling water

1/2 cup sour cream

1 teaspoon chives or 1/2 teaspoon dried

1 teaspoon fresh dill, chopped or 1/2 teaspoon dried

1 teaspoon salt

2 teaspoons sugar

Fresh ground black pepper, to taste

Lemon juice or white vinegar

1 Thinly slice cucumbers. Cover with boiling water and let stand 20 minutes.

2 Drain and plunge into cold water. Let stand a minute, drain again and refrigerate for 30 minutes.

3 Mix sour cream with sugar, pepper and chives and/or dill. Salt cucumbers well and combine with sour cream mixture. Correct the tartness with lemon juice or vinegar.

4 Chill and serve cold.

Serves 6

Anne Pustai

Fresh Refrigerator Pickles
Uborka

Pair pickled vegetables with spicy meats dishes to add a cool crunch-pleasing sensation.

3 large cucumbers, unpeeled, thinly sliced

1 medium green pepper, chopped

1 medium onion, chopped

1 tablespoon salt

1 tablespoon celery seed

3/4 cup sugar

1/2 cup white vinegar

1 Combine cucumber slices with green pepper and onion. Gently stir in salt and celery seed. Let stand about one hour at room temperature.

2 In a small, noncorrosive saucepan, combine sugar and vinegar over low heat and stir until sugar is dissolved. Cool to room temperature.

3 Pour over vegetables and stir to blend. Cover or place in appropriate noncorrosive containers.

4 Refrigerate. Pickles are ready in a few days. Store covered in refrigerator.

Yield: About 5 cups.

Anne Pustai

Freezer Sweet Pickles
Uborka

Extend the life of summer's harvest.

7 cups small cucumbers, unpeeled, thinly sliced

1-1/2 tablespoons salt

2 cups sugar

1 cup white vinegar

1-1/2 teaspoons celery seed

1 cup onions, sliced very thin

1 Salt cucumber slices; let stand 2 hours at room temperature; drain liquid and discard.

2 Bring sugar, vinegar and celery seed to a boil. Cool to room temperature.

3 Layer cucumbers alternately with onions into small non-corrosive jars. Cover with cooled liquid. Cover tightly with plastic wrap. Freeze.

4 Thaw overnight in refrigerator when ready to use.

Yield: About 6 cups

Ethel Kardar; Gizella Mayer

Summer Crock Dill Cucumbers
Kovászos uborka

This traditional heritage method for dills is still very common during sunny harvest months.

10 to 12 medium-sized cucumbers, unwaxed and skin on

3/4 gallon water (3 quarts) or to cover

2 tablespoons salt

Fresh dill, about a bunch

2 to 3 slices of rye bread, toasted

1 teaspoon flour

1 Cut ends off cucumbers and make a vertical slit, without cutting through the ends; make a quarter turn and repeat, being sure not to cut through.

2 Boil the water with salt.

3 Place the dill in the bottom of a clean gallon jar or crock. Stand the cucumbers tightly in the jar. Cover with additional dill. Pour the hot brine over the cucumbers to cover completely, sprinkle flour over top and let cool to room temperature.

4 Top with rye bread and cover with a loose lid.

5 Place in a sunny place or garden or warm place to ripen two to five days.

6 When cucumbers begin to turn yellow, remove rye bread and discard. Strain the liquid, reserve it. Place pickles back in jar, pour reserved liquid over them and transfer to refrigerator for at least a day before using.

Variation

• Place 2 cloves of garlic on the bottom and top of the jar with the dill.

In memory of Julianna Roczei

Mixed Vegetable Salad

Vegyes zöldség saláta

Layering creates a perfect and colorful mix of summer vegetables. Be sure to let the flavors mingle.

1 cup cucumbers, sliced 1/4-inch

1 cup tomatoes, sliced 1/4-inch

1 cup onions, sliced 1/4-inch

1 cup peppers, sliced 1/4-inch use red or sweet banana peppers or a mix of both

1 small clove garlic

1-1/2 cups water

1 teaspoon salt

1/4 teaspoon white pepper

1-1/2 tablespoons sugar

1/4 cup white vinegar

1 In a medium glass bowl, layer half of the cucumbers, followed by half of the tomatoes, onions and peppers. Repeat, finishing with peppers.

2 Thinly slice garlic. Pour water into a small bowl, and add garlic. Add salt, pepper, sugar and vinegar and stir until sugar is completely dissolved. Remove garlic and pour over vegetables.

3 Let stand one hour at room temperature. Pour off liquid into bowl; pour over vegetables again; pour off and pour over vegetables. Refrigerate several hours in the liquid and serve. Or if preferred, drain liquid off before serving.

In memory of Bill Koteles and with thanks to the Hungarian Reformed Federation

Summer's End Relish

Nyár végi vagdalt zöldség

Green tomatoes before the first freeze are put to use in the amalgamating flavors of this relish.

2 quarts green tomatoes

1 quart red ripe tomatoes

1/2 head green cabbage

3 red peppers

3 green peppers

3 large onions

3 stalks celery

1 large cucumber, peeled

1/2 cup salt

6 cups vinegar

1 teaspoon mustard

Freshly grated horseradish, optional

1 Chop vegetables and combine with salt. Let stand overnight and squeeze out excess liquid

2 Place vegetables, vinegar, mustard and horseradish, if using in a large saucepan. Simmer over medium heat until thickened.

3 Seal in sterilized jars.

Irene Takacs

Pickled Hungarian Hot Peppers

Erős paprika savanyúság

Everyone asks what to do with all the really hot Hungarian peppers. Pickling takes the edge off the heat.

20 to 25 Hungarian hot peppers, ends trimmed, slit lengthwise and seeded

6 teaspoons of mixed pickling spices

6 sprigs fresh dill, rinsed or

3 teaspoons dill seeds

6 cloves garlic, split

3-1/4 quarts water

3/4 quarts white vinegar

1/2 cup salt

1/4 cup sugar

1/2 teaspoon alum

1 In each of 6 clean quart jars, place 5 to 6 peppers, 1 teaspoon of pickling spices, 1 clove garlic, split and a sprig of fresh dill or 1/2 teaspoon dill seeds.

2 Heat water, vinegar, salt and sugar to simmer and add alum, stirring to dissolve. Pour over peppers.

3 Cool to room temperature and seal.

Margaret Shary

Zucchini Pickles

Cukkíni uborka

A mild squash in a spicy mixture is an excellent way to use the summer's abundance of zucchini.

5 pounds of 5 or 6-inch zucchini, unpeeled, cut into 1/4-inch slices

4 to 5 medium onions, thinly sliced

1/4 cup pickling salt

2 teaspoons celery seed

2 teaspoon turmeric

1 teaspoon dry mustard or mustard seed

2 cups sugar

4 cups distilled white vinegar or apple cider vinegar

1 Combine vinegar, sugar, salt, celery seed, turmeric and mustard in medium saucepan. Bring to a boil and simmer 3 minutes. Pour over zucchini and onions and let stand one hour, stirring occasionally.

2 Remove vegetables and strain liquid.

3 In each of 6 clean pint jars, place zucchini and onions. Pour strained liquid within 1/2-inch of top of jar, making sure liquid completely covers the zucchini.

4 Cool uncovered jars to room temperature. Seal.

Makes 6 pints

Ella Hegyi

Eggplant Fritters

Rántott padlizsán

Doesn't everyone use this recipe? Our moms did when we brought eggplants from Harvey Rice gardens at East 116th Street and Buckeye Road.

1 large eggplant, skin on, sliced into thin rounds

2 eggs

2 cups flour

1 cup milk

1 teaspoon salt

Oil for frying

1 Sprinkle eggplant with salt; let stand 20 minutes.

2 In a shallow bowl, whisk egg, flour, salt and milk. Blot eggplant slices dry with paper towels and dip into egg mixture.

3 In a large deep skillet or deep fryer, heat oil until hot and fry eggplant slices until golden. Remove and drain on paper towel. Sprinkle with grated Parmesan or cheddar cheese.

Barb Rayer

Kohlrabi and Carrot and Slaw

Karalábé és sárgarépa saláta

These two vegetables pair well together both raw and cooked. This version packs extra crunch.

1 pound kohlrabi

1 medium carrot

2 tablespoons fresh chopped dill

1 tablespoon salt

2 cloves garlic, minced

1 teaspoon sugar

2 tablespoons white vinegar

3 tablespoons olive or canola oil

1 Peel kohlrabi, grate on large hole of grater Toss with 1 teaspoon salt, and let stand in strainer over bowl for about 30 minutes. Rinse lightly and pat dry. Peel and grate carrot on large hole of grater. Combine in bowl.

2 Mix oil, vinegar, garlic and sugar. Pour over kohlrabi and carrots and toss with dill. Chill before serving. Season with salt and pepper to taste.

Serves 4

Mark Shary

Kohlrabi with Butter

Vajas karalábé

Kohlrabi has a distinctive place in Hungarian cooking. It has undertones of cucumber and radish flavors.

3 young, green kohlrabi, peeled and sliced or shredded

2 tablespoons butter or olive oil

Salt and pepper, to taste

1 In a 1 quart saucepan, bring salted water to a boil and add kohlrabi, bring to a simmer and cook until tender, about 10 minutes, less if you prefer a crisper vegetable. Drain.

2 Over very low heat, add butter to saucepan. Flavor melted butter with marjoram, caraway, onion, dill, thyme or ginger or leave plain. Toss in kohlrabi, stirring to coat. Season to taste.

Serves 4

Mashed Lentils

Lencsepüré

A filling and flavorful alternative to mashed potatoes, mashed lentils mingle well with bacon and onion flavors.

1 pound lentils, washed and sorted

2 quarts water

1 teaspoon salt

1/4 pound piece of bacon

1 large onion, sliced

2 tablespoons bacon fat

2 tablespoons flour

Salt and pepper, to taste

1 In a 4-quart soup pot, cook lentils with bacon in salted water until lentils are tender and thickened. Add a little water if necessary to keep from scorching.

2 Remove from heat and sprinkle flour on lentils. Mash until the lentils are the consistency of mashed potatoes.

3 In a separate small saucepan, brown the onion in bacon fat and stir into lentils; stir lightly. Season to taste and cook until well blended, about 5 minutes.

Serves 6

Ethel Kardar

Stewed Peppers, Onions & Tomatoes
Lecsó

Lecsó is the most colorful and versatile cooked Hungarian vegetable dish. It may be used as a flavoring element in stews or sauces, served as a side dish, or a topping for potatoes or tarhonya.

1 large yellow onion, or 4 small yellow onions, finely chopped

4 large, fresh, ripe tomatoes, quartered, about 1-1/4 pounds

1-1/2 pounds peppers: cored, trimmed and cut in 1/2-inch strips, lengthwise, preferably mixed peppers with sweet green, yellow and red and part hot Hungarian banana peppers

1 tablespoon paprika

2 teaspoons sugar, to taste, optional

3 tablespoons oil or bacon fat, though lard was traditional

1 Heat pan and fat, add onions, and cook over low heat until translucent. Remove from heat and add paprika and stir. Add peppers and salt and cover. Simmer for 10-15 minutes.

2 Add tomatoes, sugar (if using) and cook over low heat, stewing until soft, about 10 minutes for textured vegetables or 20 minutes, for stewed.

Serve as a side dish or a lunch with good bread or mixed with *tarhonya* or *kolbász* sausage.

Variations

- Tomatoes may be scalded and skins removed.
- Garlic may be added with the onions.
- Black pepper, bay leaf or thyme may be used to season.
- See page 67 for a *lecsó* recipe with *kolbász*.

Serves 6-8

Hungarian Scalloped Potatoes

Rakottkrumpli

Good for a buffet for a large gathering, the ease of preparation defies the richness of the flavors.

6 medium potatoes
(4 pounds)

8 hard-cooked eggs, sliced

1/4 pound (1 stick) butter, divided

3/4 cup dry bread crumbs

1/2 cup sour cream

Salt and pepper, to taste

1 Boil potatoes until tender or skewer goes through smoothly, about 20 minutes. Drain, cool and slice 1/4-inch thick.

2 Melt 2 tablespoons of the butter and coat the bottom of a baking dish. Sprinkle with some of the bread crumbs.

3 Layer potatoes, then eggs, salt and pepper, and crumbs. Dot with butter. Continue layering until all ingredients are used.

4 Spoon sour cream over the top. Sprinkle with bread crumbs.

5 Bake at 350° for 45 to 60 minutes or until golden brown.

Variations

• 1-1/2 pound smoked *kolbász* or ham, sliced to 1/4-inch may be placed on top of potato layers.

• Sour cream may be increased to 1 cup.

Serves 6-8

In memory of Irene Dono,
Also in memory of Margie Csolty

Potatoes Paprikas

Paprikás krumpli

This creamy side dish is everyone's favorite – the ultimate Hungarian potato comfort food.

4 to 6 raw potatoes, peeled and sliced about 1/8-inch thick

2 onions, chopped or sliced

3 tablespoons shortening or 1 tablespoon oil or bacon drippings

1 tablespoon paprika

1/2 cup water

Salt and pepper, to taste

1 In a dutch oven or heavy skillet, melt shortening. Add onions and cook and stir until golden. Add paprika, sliced potatoes, salt and pepper. Stir to coat potatoes. Fry until evenly browned, about 10 minutes.

2 Add water, stir and cover tightly and cook 15 minutes over medium low heat, stirring occasionally. Uncover and simmer until potatoes are completely tender and there is about 1/4 cup liquid left in pan.

Variations

• Sliced *kolbász* may be added. 1/4 teaspoon chili powder, caraway seed are other flavor additions.

• Cook until edges of potatoes become crispy.

Irene Kita, Elizabeth Robinson, and in memory of Irene Dono

Potato Pancakes

Tócsni

Soaking the potatoes extracts extra starch and the baking powder makes the pancakes a bit lighter.

3 cups grated potatoes (peeled prior to grating)

2 eggs, well beaten

1-1/2 tablespoons flour

1/8 teaspoon baking powder

1 teaspoon salt

1/2 teaspoon onion juice

1 Peel potatoes and place in a large bowl. Cover potatoes with cold water. Let stand for 12 hours. Pour off water and grate potatoes to yield 3 cups. Drain well.

2 Place grated potatoes in bowl, add eggs and mix lightly. Stir in remaining ingredients. Drop from tablespoon into hot, well-greased skillet. Brown on both sides. Serve with applesauce and crisp bacon.

Variation

• Use 1 tablespoon minced onion instead of onion juice.

Julianna Kovach Zingale, in memory of Sophia Kovach

Potato Pancakes with Caraway

Köménymagos tócsni

A side dish, lunch or late night snack.

6 medium potatoes,

1 small onion

2 slightly beaten eggs

3 tablespoons flour

1/2 teaspoon pepper

1 teaspoon salt

1 teaspoon caraway seed

1 Gently toast the caraway seed in a small frying pan or in a toaster oven until fragrant.

2 Peel potatoes and grate with onion. Let drain 10 minutes. Stir in eggs, flour, salt and pepper.

3 Drop by spoonfuls onto hot, greased skillet. Brown on both sides over medium heat. Drain on paper towel. Serve with applesauce.

In memory of Irene Schnierer

Hungarian Creamed Spinach

Magyaros spenótfőzelék

Traditionally a creamy-mellow spinach dish, the spicy variation livens up any meal.

1 pound spinach or one small box frozen, chopped spinach

1/2 cup water

2 tablespoons butter

2 tablespoons flour

1/2 cup sour cream

Salt and pepper, to taste

Hard-cooked eggs, optional

1 Bring water to boil and add salt. Add spinach cook until tender. Drain, reserving liquid. Cool. Chop spinach finely.

2 Melt butter; add flour, stirring and brown lightly. Add spinach liquid and stir with whisk to form smooth sauce. Add to chopped spinach; stir in sour cream; add salt to taste. Garnish with hard-boiled eggs.

Variations

• 1 teaspoon sweet paprika may be added to the sauce.

• Sour cream may be enhanced with 1/2 teaspoon minced onion and/or a small clove of minced garlic. 1/2 tablespoon prepared horseradish can also be added to the sour cream.

Serves 4

In memory of Olga Kish

Sweet Vinaigrette Salad Dressing

Ecetes saláta izesito

Slightly sweet, slightly astringent, this light vinaigrette is more popular than oil and vinegar.

1/4 cup
white vinegar,
to taste

1/2 cup water

2 tablespoons sugar

Thoroughly mix sugar in the water and add the vinegar before tossing with salad. Add more or less vinegar to taste.

Variation

• Add a 1 tablespoon of oil to the mix.

Wilted lettuce

Dinsztelt saláta

Hungarians love bacon fat and here is another way to use it. Hot meets cold with a sizzle!

Green and/or red
leaf lettuce, arranged
on serving plates

3 strips bacon,
chopped 1/4-inch

1/4 cup water

1/2 cup vinegar

2 tablespoons sugar

1/2 teaspoon salt

1 clove garlic, finely
chopped

1 Fry the bacon and remove from fat. Drain on paper towel. Cool the fat slightly.

2 Add the sugar, salt, garlic, water and vinegar to the fat and bring to a boil.

3 Arrange the lettuce on salad plates and pour hot dressing over the lettuce. Cool a bit. Garnish with crumbled bacon. Serve with good crusty bread.

Hubbard Squash Strudel

Tökös rétes

Savory strudel can be eaten as a warm appetizer or as a light lunch or as an after dinner treat.

1 package Athens® phyllo dough or homemade strudel dough

3 pounds Hubbard Squash (available in autumn)

1/2 cup sugar

2 teaspoons cinnamon

1-1/2 pounds (6 sticks) butter or margarine, melted

2 cups bread crumbs

1/2 teaspoon black pepper

1 Follow directions on phyllo dough box for thawing. Use 4 sheets of dough per roll of strudel.

2 Peel squash. Grate on the large holes of a four-sided grater.

3 In a large bowl, mix squash, cinnamon, sugar and pepper.

4 Brush each of four sheets of dough with butter. Stack evenly and spread 1/4 of the squash filling over dough and fold from wide end in about 3 to 4-inch widths. Place on baking sheet, seam side down. Brush with melted butter.

5 Repeat 3 times, each using 4 sheets of phyllo and 1/4 of the squash filling.

6 Bake at 350° for 30 minutes until light brown. While warm, cut each roll into six pieces. Cool and dust with confectioner's sugar.

Serves 8

Helen Gyerman

122

Squash in Sour Cream

Tejfeles tök

A delicious, classic Hungarian way to use the plentiful zucchini harvest.

3 pounds zucchini or other summer squash, peeled and shredded or sliced thinly

1/2 cup chopped onion

2 tablespoons oil or shortening

2 teaspoons paprika

1 cup water

1 teaspoon salt, or to taste

2 tablespoons cornstarch

2 tablespoons milk

1 cup sour cream

2 teaspoons vinegar

1 In a large pan, cook onion in oil until golden, stirring frequently. Add paprika, stir, and mix in squash, water and salt.

2 Bring mixture to a boil over medium high heat, then reduce heat and simmer gently for 10 minutes. Squash should retain texture.

3 In a small bowl, dissolve cornstarch in milk and stir into sour cream, mixing thoroughly.

4 Pour over squash and stir to combine. Add vinegar and simmer gently until hot.

Variation

• 2 tablespoon finely chopped fresh dill or 1/4 teaspoon of dill seed may be added.

Serves 4-6

Violet Sarosi

Cheese Biscuits — *Sajtos pogácsa*, page 132

BREADS & SPREADS

Fried Dough – *Lángos*, page 134

BREAD SYMBOLIZES THE BODY OF CHRIST, THE BREAD OF LIFE. THE SPIRITUAL SIGNIFICANCE OF THE WHEAT HARVEST IS SO CENTRAL TO HUNGARIAN CULTURE THAT IT IS CELEBRATED IN THE REFORMED FAITH AT THE THANKSGIVING FOR THE NEW BREAD COMMUNION. BREAD IS CENTRAL TO THE HUNGARIAN DINNER TABLE AS WELL. IN THE OLD WORLD, EACH VILLAGE USED WHEAT MILLED LOCALLY, OFTEN MIXING IT WITH RYE FLOUR, CORNMEAL OR POTATO FLOUR TO CREATE A DENSE, FULL-BODIED LOAF, LEAVENED WITH YEAST SPONGE STARTER HANDED DOWN THROUGH GENERATIONS. A CONSTANT ACCOMPANIMENT TO MEALS, BREAD HAS ALWAYS BEEN USED TO SOAK UP SAUCES. BUT IT IS ALSO USED TO CATCH THE BACON DRIPPINGS FOR *SZALONNA* AND AS THE WRAP FOR *KOLBÁSZ* SANDWICHES. AND IT MAKES GREAT TOAST, ESPECIALLY WHEN TOPPED WITH HOMEMADE FRUIT PRESERVES.

Hungarian White Bread from Starter

Magyar fehér kenyér

In Hungary, starter was begun from naturally-occurring grape yeast. Here's an version that doesn't require a vineyard.

Starter

2 cups bread flour

1-1/4 cups water, room temperature

1 teaspoon salt

1/2 teaspoon rapid rise dry yeast

Bread

4-1/2 cups bread flour

2 teaspoons salt

2 tablespoons sugar

1/4 cup solid vegetable shortening

2 teaspoons rapid rise dry yeast

1-1/4 cups water, room temperature

1 *Day 1, make starter* In a mixer fitted with a paddle attachment, place water, salt and yeast and blend thoroughly. Add flour and mix 3 minutes. Pour into a slightly oversized bowl, cover and refrigerate overnight.

2 *Day 2* Bring starter to room temperature, about 2 hours.

3 In a separate bowl, mix flour and salt.

4 In the mixer with the paddle attachment, place starter mixture, shortening, yeast and water. Blend slowly until an elastic dough forms.

5 Add half of the flour mixture and blend about 1 minute until the flour is incorporated. With dough hook, add remaining flour and mix until dough forms a sticky ball.

6 Place dough on lightly floured board and knead for about 3 minutes, adding flour as necessary until dough forms a smooth ball.

7 Place dough in lightly oiled 4-quart bowl. Cover and let rise in a warm place until doubled, about 1-1/2 hours. Punch and shape into 2 loaves that fit 9-1/4 x 5-1/4 x 2-3/4-inch pans. Cover and let rise again, until dough crests 1/2-inch over the pan's edge, about 1-1/2 hours. *Preheat oven to 350° during the last rising.*

8 Bake at center of oven for 40 minutes. Remove loaves from pans and cool on rack.

Makes 2 loaves

Mark Shary

Hungarian Rye Bread
Magyar rozskenyér

Rye was widely cultivated in Northern Hungary. The bread is an essential accompaniment to soups, szalonna and sopping up juices.

1 cup milk, room temperature

2-1/3 cups water

2-1/2 teaspoons rapid rise yeast

3-1/2 cups unbleached bread flour

2-1/2 cups rye flour

2 teaspoons salt

2 tablespoons caraway seed

2 tablespoons honey

1 teaspoon dill seeds, optional

1 Crush caraway seeds in mortar and pestle or spice grinder. In a small saucepan, bring water and seeds to a boil. Reduce heat and simmer 5 minutes. Remove from heat and let stand 30 minutes. Strain and reserve liquid. Cool to room temperature. Discard seeds.

2 Mix unbleached bread flour, rye flour, salt and dill seeds, if using.

3 In a mixer fitted with a paddle attachment, pour in water, honey, milk and mix. Add yeast and blend. Add 3 cups flour mixture and mix completely.

4 With dough hook attachment, add remaining flour and mix until dough forms a slightly sticky ball.

5 Place dough on lightly floured board and knead for about 3 minutes, adding flour as necessary until dough forms a smooth ball.

6 Place dough in lightly oiled 4-quart bowl. Cover and let rise in a warm place until doubled, about 1-1/2 hours. Punch and shape into 2 loaves that fit slightly smaller than the 9-1/4 x 5-1/4 x 2-3/4-inch pans. Let rise, covered, in a warm place, until dough crests 1/2-inch over the edge of the pan, about 1-1/2 hours.

Preheat oven to 350°.

7 Bake at center of oven for 40 minutes. Remove loaves from pans and cool on rack.

Makes 2 loaves

Potato Bread

Krumplis kenyér

The potato adds a natural sweetness, body and texture to this bread which is also great for toast.

1 pound
russet potatoes,
washed and peeled

2 cups reserved
liquid from cooking
potato, lukewarm

1-1/2 tablespoons
dry yeast

1/4 teaspoon sugar

1 tablespoon
kosher salt

7-1/2 cups
bread flour

1 teaspoon flour

1 In a saucepan, boil the potatoes in 1-1/2 quarts of water. Reserve 2 cups of the potato water and cool to lukewarm.

2 Mash the potatoes and set aside to cool to lukewarm.

3 Proof yeast by sprinkling it over 1/4 cup of the reserved, warm (100-115° F.) potato water with a 1/4 teaspoon of sugar. Set aside in a warm place for 5 to 10 minutes, until mixture bubbles.

4 In a bowl of a mixer fitted with a dough hook, place mashed potatoes, yeast mixture and remaining potato water. Blend on low speed 1 minute. Add 5 cups of the flour and mix until dough begins to come away from the sides and bottom of the bowl. Continue to add flour, a tablespoon at a time if the dough is very sticky.

5 Turn dough onto a floured board and knead for several minutes. Dough will be slightly sticky. Divide into two equal portions.

6 Lightly oil two 9 x 5 x 3-inch pans and place dough in pans. Dust tops with 1 teaspoon flour. Cover with a dry towel and let rise until dough crests about 1-inch above the pan edge.

Preheat oven to 450°

7 Bake 10 minutes; reduce heat to 375° and continue to bake for about 25 minutes longer.

8 Remove from pans and cool completely.

Makes 2 loaves

Crackling Biscuits #1

Tepertős pogácsa

Flaky and tender, the wine adds its nuance of flavor to this savory snack.

6 cups flour

1 tablespoon salt

2 heaping tablespoons shortening

2 ounces fresh yeast

1/2 cup sour cream

2 eggs

1 cup white wine, warmed

1 pound cracklings, ground fine

1 In a large bowl, mix shortening with flour. In a separate bowl, beat eggs and sour cream together. Add to dry ingredients followed by yeast and wine to make soft dough. Beat well. Let rise for 1 hour.

2 Roll dough as thin as possible. Spread half of crackling across surface of dough. Fold one third of dough to center and other third over the center; spread remaining crackling; fold again. Cover with bowl and let rest 30 minutes.

3 Roll dough out again; repeat. Spread and fold. Cover and let rest 30 minutes. Roll again. Spread and fold until all of the crackling is used. Let rest 30 minutes; roll and cut with a biscuit cutter or a glass. Place on baking sheet. Score tops of biscuits with a knife.

4 Let rise for 30 minutes; brush with egg wash.

Preheat oven to 375°

5 Bake for 30 minutes.

In memory of Julia Szonyi

Hungarian Tea Biscuits #2

Tepertős pogácsa

Pogácsa make great little snacks any time of the day.

5 cups sifted cake flour

3 tablespoons plus 1 teaspoon sugar

2 teaspoons salt

3/8 pound (1-1/4 sticks) butter, softened

2 cakes yeast (.06 oz each.)

1 cup lukewarm milk

4 egg yolks

1/4 teaspoon vanilla

3/4 cup cracklings or crumbled bacon

1 egg, lightly beaten

1 Sift flour, sugar and salt. Cut in butter until the consistency of cornmeal. Crumble yeast into warm milk and let soften 3 minutes.

2 Beat in egg yolks and vanilla. Slowly add to flour/butter mixture. Work in cracklings. Let rest 15 minutes so dough becomes firm enough to roll.

3 On lightly floured surface, roll dough to a 1/2-inch thick rectangle. Brush with beaten egg. Fold over dough, roll again to 1/2-inch thick; brush with egg. Fold over double and chill 15 minutes. Repeat twice, chilling 15 minutes between each handling. After last chilling, roll dough out to 3/4-inch thick. Brush with egg. Score both ways on diagonal, about 1/8-inch apart. Cut with biscuit cutter or glass. Place on greased baking sheet.

Preheat oven to 375°.

4 Let biscuits rise on for 20 minutes. Bake for 12 to 15 minutes.

Anne Pustai

Butter Biscuits

Vajas pogácsa

A rich dough, the cold butter yields an exceptionally flaky and quick biscuit.

3/4 pound (3 sticks) butter, frozen

3 egg yolks and 3 egg whites, slightly beaten

3 cups flour

3 tablespoons sugar

1 cup sour cream

2 teaspoons baking powder

1/8 teaspoon salt

Preheat oven to 400°

1 In a large bowl, mix flour, salt, sugar and baking powder. Grate frozen butter into the bowl and mix. In a separate bowl, whisk sour cream and egg yolks then add to flour mixture. Knead into a smooth dough.

2 On a floured surface, roll dough to 1/4-inch thick and fold in thirds. Roll to 1/2-inch thick. Score dough crisscross and cut with 1-inch biscuit cutter, or cut 1-1/2-inch strips with a pastry wheel. Place on cookie sheet. Brush with egg whites.

3 Bake at 400° for 5 minutes and reduce heat to 350°, baking until golden, about 10 minutes.

Rachel Smith

Cheese Biscuits

Sajtos pogácsa

The Parmesan adds a salty, savory taste to this basic biscuit.

4 cups flour

3/4 pound (3 sticks) cold margarine

3 egg yolks

3 tablespoons sugar

1/2 pint sour cream

1/2 cup milk

2 teaspoons baking powder

1/2 teaspoons salt

2 tablespoons grated Parmesan cheese

Preheat oven to 400°

1 In a medium bowl, cut margarine into flour. Mix together egg yolks, sugar, sour cream, milk baking powder, salt and cheese and add to the margarine-flour mixture. Wrap in plastic wrap and refrigerate for at least 4 hours or overnight.

2 Roll out to 1/2-inch thick and cut with 1-inch biscuit cutter or cut into strips with knife or pastry wheel.

3 Bake for 20 to 25 minutes until golden.

In memory of Olga Kish

Potato Biscuits

Krumplis pogácsa

Warm, slathered with butter and a dab of fruit preserves, this a satisfying brunch or breakfast biscuit.

3/4 pound (3 sticks) butter

3 egg yolks

3 cups flour

3 tablespoons sugar

1 cup sour cream

1/2 cup milk

2 teaspoons baking powder

Pinch salt

1 medium potato

1 Cook potato, drain liquid and mash. Cool.

Preheat oven to 400°

2 Cut butter into flour until crumbly. Mix with baking powder and sugar. Add sour cream and yolks. Work into smooth dough.

3 Roll to about 1/4-inch thickness and cut with biscuit cutter or glass. Brush top with egg white and make crisscross slashes with knife.

4 Bake for 5 minutes. Reduce heat to 350° and bake to golden brown, about 15 to 20 minutes.

Fried Dough

Lángos

The potato adds a natural sweetness, body and texture to this fried bread.

4 medium potatoes, peeled

1-1/2 –2 cups flour

1 ounce fresh yeast

1 teaspoon sugar

1/2 teaspoon salt

1/2 cup warm milk

2 eggs

1-1/2 cups warm water

Vegetable oil for frying

1 Cook the potatoes in boiling water until tender, about 20 minutes; drain, mash. and cool slightly.

2 In a medium bowl, dissolve the yeast and sugar in the lukewarm milk. Set aside until it bubbles, about 10 minutes.

3 In a large bowl, sift flour and salt. Add mashed potatoes. Make a well in the center and pour in yeast mixture. Knead dough until it is smooth, about 5 to 7 minutes.

Place dough in a large oiled bowl and cover with a towel to rise until doubled in size, about 1 hour.

4 Roll or pat pieces of the dough into 1/2-inch thick rounds about 5-inch in diameter on a floured board.

5 In a deep skillet, heat 2 inches of oil until hot. Fry dough, one at time until golden, turn carefully and fry opposite side. Lift from oil, shake off excess and finish draining on paper towels.

6 Sprinkle with confectioner's sugar, salt, pepper or garlic salt or rub with a clove of cut garlic and a shake of paprika. Always serve warm.

Priscilla Wargo

Walnut Dinner Rolls

Dío Zsemle

Walnut rolls can be served with dinner or as an after-dinner roll with coffee.

5 egg yolks, room temperature

1 cup margarine, room temperature

1 cup lukewarm cream

1 large cake of yeast

1/4 teaspoon sugar

3 cups flour

1 cup chopped nuts

Sugar for board

1 Proof yeast by crumbling it into 2 tablespoons of the warm cream (100-115° F.) mixed with 1/4 teaspoon of sugar. Set aside in a warm place about 3 to 5 minutes until mixture bubbles.

2 Cream butter thoroughly. Add eggs, one at a time and pour in yeast. Gradually add flour and beat until dough pulls away from sides of bowl.

3 Refrigerate overnight, or at least 3 hours.

4 Spread pastry board with sugar and nuts. Roll out the dough, thinly and then roll up like a jelly roll. Cut into 1/2-inch slices.

5 Place on cookie sheet and let rise for 1 hour.

Preheat oven to 350°

6 Bake rolls 15 to 20 minutes.

Margaret Jacob

Liptauer Cheese Spread

Liptói turó körözött

Liptauer is a sharp sheep's milk cheese but cream cheese approximates its consistency. Served with a good bread, this spread is served at lunch or dinner.

8 ounces Liptauer cheese or 8 ounces cream cheese

1/2 cup (1 stick) butter, softened

3 tablespoons sour cream

1 tablespoons finely chopped onion or chives

1 tablespoon prepared mustard

1-1/2 teaspoon paprika

1 teaspoon caraway seed

1/2 teaspoon salt

12 parsley sprigs

12 anchovy fillets, rinsed, optional

1 In a bowl, cream butter, cheese, and sour cream.

2 Add onion or chives, mustard, paprika, caraway seed and salt and mix well.

3 Shape into smooth mound and transfer to serving plate. Refrigerate for 1 to 2 hours. Sprinkle with paprika. Garnish plate with parsley and rolled anchovy fillets, if using.

4 Spread on rye bread.

Variations

• 4 ounces each dry cottage cheese and cream cheese, mixed may be substituted for the Liptauer.

• 8 ounces of cream cheese may be substituted for the Liptauer. Butter may be omitted.

• 1 or 2 cloves of minced garlic may be added with the onion.

In memory of Rt. Rev. Dr. Stephen Szabo

Easter Cheese Ball

Húsvéti sajtos golyó

Typically served with Easter dinner, this is a sweet cheese.

1 dozen eggs

1/4 teaspoon salt

1 cup sugar

1-1/2 quarts milk

2 teaspoons vanilla

1/2 cup golden raisins, optional

1 In a bowl, whisk eggs with sugar and salt.

2 In a 4 quart saucepan, heat milk, stirring constantly, just to boiling point. Add egg-sugar mixture, vanilla and raisins, if using. Continue cooking and stirring until mixture starts to thicken and forms curds. Do not scorch.

3 Pour into dampened cloth bag or cheese cloth and squeeze to drain. Tie opening tightly and hang over a bowl and let drain overnight. Refrigerate until ready to serve.

Variations

- For a less sweet variation, use 1/2 cup sugar.

- Sprinkle with 1/2 teaspoon cinnamon.

Violet Sarosi; Betty Hartman

Chocolate Butter Sponge Torte – *Csokis-vajas piskóta torta*, page 144

CAKES & TORTES

White Cake Roll – *Fehér tekercs,*
page 147

LUXURIOUS, LAVISH, LUSCIOUS AND LAYERED, CAKES AND
TORTES WERE INSPIRED BY THE CREATIONS OF VIENNESE
PASTRY CHEFS DURING HUNGARY'S BELLE ÉPOQUE. THE
PERIOD USHERED IN A NEW HIGHBROW WAY OF ENJOYING
SWEETS: AT THE URBAN COFFEEHOUSE — USUALLY AT MIDDAY
— ACCOMPANIED BY STRONG, DARK COFFEE THAT OFFSET THE
RICH SWEETNESS. TO THIS DAY, WE RELY ON FINE BAKERS
FOR ELABORATELY LAYERED TORTES, INCLUDING THE CLASSIC
DOBOS TORTE. MANY DELICIOUS CAKES, HOWEVER, CAN
BE BAKED AND ENJOYED AT HOME. SPONGE CAKE LAYERS,
SANDWICHED WITH FILLINGS OF CREAM OR GROUND NUTS
AND ICED WITH BUTTERCREAM FROSTING, ARE AN ELEGANT
FINISH TO ANY MEAL.

Angel Sponge Cake
Piskóta

Sponge cakes provide the base for infinite varieties of desserts. As the name implies, this one is divine.

1-1/2 cups sifted cake flour

3/4 cup sugar

1/2 teaspoon baking powder

Pinch salt

6 eggs, separated, at room temperature

1/2 cup sugar

1/2 cup cold water

3/4 teaspoon cream of tartar

1 teaspoon vanilla

1/2 teaspoon almond extract

Preheat oven to 350°

1 In a large bowl, sift cake flour, sugar, baking powder and salt together five times.

2 Beat egg yolks until light and lemon-colored. Gradually add 3/4 cup sugar, until combined. Add vanilla and almond extracts.

3 In a separate bowl, beat egg whites and cream of tartar until peaks stand.

4 Into the egg yolk mixture, add the dry ingredients with the cold water; slowly add to the beaten egg whites with wire whisk, blending well.

5 Pour into ungreased tube pan. Bake for 1 hour. Turn pan upside-down to cool. When cool remove cake very gently. Serve with fruit.

In memory of Evelyn Komyati Unger

Apple Walnut Cake

Diós-almás sütemény

Apples are both Hungary's and American's, biggest fruit crops.

3 cups
coarsely grated
apples, such as
Jonathan or Golden
Delicious

1 cup sugar

3 eggs

1/2 cup oil

2 cups sifted flour

2 teaspoons vanilla

1-1/2 teaspoons
baking powder

1/2 teaspoon
baking soda

1/2 teaspoon salt

1/2 cup
chopped walnuts

Grease and flour 13 x 9-inch pan
Preheat oven to 350°

1 In a large bowl, beat eggs well and add sugar gradually. Add oil and vanilla; beat well.

2 In a separate bowl, sift dry ingredients together 2 or 3 times. Fold the dry ingredients into the egg mixture. Mix in grated apples and nuts. Bake in prepared pan at 30 to 35 minutes.

3 Cool and sprinkle with confectioner's sugar before serving.

In memory of Evelyn Komyati Unger

141

Cherry Cake

Cseresznyés lepény

Tart cherries, cinnamon and almond create a sweet aroma while baking and sheer delight in eating.

1/2 cup washed, pitted and halved tart cherries

1/4 cup brown sugar

1/2 cup milk

1 package dry yeast

5 eggs, separated

1/4 pound (1 stick) butter, cut into pieces and softened

1 cup sugar

2 cups sifted flour

1/2 cup sliced almonds

1 teaspoon vanilla

1/4 teaspoon almond extract

1 tablespoon cinnamon-sugar

Preheat oven to 350°.
Butter and flour a Bundt pan

1 Mix cherries and brown sugar and place in the bottom of the prepared pan.

2 In a small saucepan, warm milk over low heat to 115° (lukewarm). Remove from heat and sprinkle yeast over surface. Set aside.

3 In a medium bowl, beat egg whites until they stand in soft peaks. Set aside.

4 In a large bowl, beat butter and sugar until light and fluffy. Stir in egg yolks and yeast mixture, alternating with the flour. Fold in sliced almonds and, then the vanilla, almond extract and egg whites.

5 Pour the batter carefully into the prepared pan, being careful not to disturb the cherries. Bake for 50 to 60 minutes or until the cake pulls away from the sides of the pan or until a cake tester comes out clean.

6 Run a knife around the edge of the pan and invert over a cake rack. Sprinkle with cinnamon-sugar. Serve warm or cool.

Variation

• Bake in a 9-inch round layer cake pan. Increase the cherries so the entire bottom of the pan will be covered. Bake at 350° for 50 minutes or until cake tester comes out clean.

Violet Sarosi/American Hungarian Foundation

Maraschino Cherry Cake

Maraschinós-cseresznyés kalács

Kuchens, sweet cakes filled with fruit or nuts, are German; they filtered to Hungary through Vienna.

1 cup sugar

1/4 pound (1 stick) butter

2 eggs

2 cups sifted flour

1 teaspoon baking powder

1 teaspoon baking soda

1 teaspoon vanilla

1/2 pint sour cream

Filling

18 maraschino cherries, cut fine

3/4 cup nuts

1/4 cup sugar

1 teaspoon cinnamon

Grease a 10-inch tube pan

Preheat oven to 350°

1 Combine filling ingredients in a small bowl and set aside.

2 Combine flour, baking powder, baking soda in a medium bowl and set aside.

3 In a large bowl, cream sugar and butter; add eggs. Stir in dry ingredients, sour cream and vanilla. Mix until smooth.

4 Spread half the batter into the bottom of the prepared tube pan. Sprinkle half the filling over the dough; layer the rest of the dough over the filling and sprinkle the remaining filling on the top of the dough.

5 Bake 30 to 35 minutes.

Violet Sarosi, and in memories of Julia Szonyi, Irene Waszil

143

Chocolate Butter Sponge Torte

Csokis-vajas piskóta torta

This light cake is deserving of the extra time spent on the frosting, which truly is the "icing on the cake."

1/2 pound (2 sticks) unsalted butter

6 eggs, separated

Juice and zest of 1 lemon

2 teaspoons baking powder

2 cups flour

1 cup sugar

1/2 German Chocolate bar, grated (3 ounces Sweet Chocolate)

Frosting

4 ounces unsweetened chocolate, cut into pieces

2 tablespoons hot water

1 cup confectioner's sugar

2 eggs, well beaten

1/2 cup (1 stick) unsalted butter, cut into 1-inch chunks

Preheat oven to 350°.

1 In a large bowl, cream butter, sugar and egg yolks. Add flour, baking powder, lemon juice and zest. Fold in chocolate.

2 Beat egg whites to stiff peaks and fold into batter. Spread in 13 x 9-inch pan or two 8-inch round cake pans.

3 Bake for 35 minutes. Cool.

Frosting

1 Melt chocolate in the top of a double boiler. Add hot water and blend.

2 Add eggs and sugar. Blend thoroughly. Remove pan from heat but keep mixture over the hot water. Stir constantly until mixture thickens, about 3 minutes.

3 Prepare an ice bath (half water, half ice) in a large bowl. Place top of double boiler pan into the ice bath and stir chocolate occasionally until mixture becomes lukewarm.

4 Add butter, 2 tablespoons at a time, stirring until incorporated each time.

5 Refrigerate until ready to use or spread on cooled cake.

Violet Sarosi

Chocolate Cake

Csokoládés sütemény

Everyone needs a good chocolate cake!

1/2 cup shortening, softened	*Preheat oven to 350°.*
1 cup sugar	*Two 9-inch round cake pans, greased and floured or lined with waxed paper or parchment*

1/2 cup shortening,
softened

1 cup sugar

1 teaspoon salt

1 teaspoon vanilla

1 cup water

2-1/2 cups cake flour

1/2 cup cocoa

1/3 cup cold water

1-1/2 teaspoons
baking soda

1/3 cup water

3 egg whites,
yolks discarded

3/4 cup sugar

Frosting

1/2 pint
heavy cream

1/2 pint cream (25%)

1 cup
confectioner's sugar

1 teaspoon vanilla

5 tablespoons cocoa

Preheat oven to 350°.
Two 9-inch round cake pans, greased and floured or lined with waxed paper or parchment

1 In a large bowl, cream shortening and sugar. Add salt and vanilla.

2 In a separate cup, combine cocoa and 1/3 cup cold water until smooth. Beat cocoa into creamed mixture. Add flour alternating with 1 cup water.

3 In a medium bowl, beat egg whites until soft peaks form; gradually add sugar and continue beating until stiff peaks form. Gently fold egg whites into batter.

4 Combine baking soda with 1/3 cup water and stir into batter, mixing well. Pour into prepared cake pans. Bake for 50 minutes, until cake pulls away from edges of pan and tests clean with a toothpick. Cool and frost.

Chocolate Whipped Cream Frosting.

1 Mix all frosting ingredients together, but do not beat. Refrigerate about 2 hours.

2 Beat until smooth and spread on cake. Refrigerate any unused portion.

Louise Lucheck, in memory of Julia Szonyi

Cocoa Roll

Kakaós tekercs

A luscious chocolate cake roll filled with chocolate buttercream and finished with a dusting of cocoa.

5 eggs, separated

3/4 cup sugar

1/4 cup flour

1/2 teaspoon baking powder

1/2 teaspoon vanilla

1/4 cup cocoa

1/2 teaspoon salt

Buttercream Filling

3/8 pound (1-1/2 sticks) unsalted butter, softened

1-1/2 cups confectioner's sugar

Milk

4 tablespoons unsweetened cocoa

1 tablespoon unsweetened cocoa for finish

Grease and flour a 15 x 10 x 1-inch pan or line with parchment paper.
Preheat oven to 375°.

1 In a large bowl, beat egg yolks until frothy. Add sugar and beat well until lemon-colored.

2 Sift together flour, baking powder, salt and cocoa. Gently stir into yolk mixture. Add vanilla.

3 In a separate bowl, beat the egg whites until soft peaks form. Fold into batter.

4 Spread batter onto prepared pan. Bake 12 to 15 minutes.

5 Place a clean, dry dish towel on top of the cake and invert pan. If parchment was used to line pan, gently peel off paper and discard. Beginning at the narrow end, roll the cake (and towel) into a spiral, jelly-roll style. Cool.

6 When completely cool, prepare filling. Unroll cake, spread with filling and roll. Sift the one tablespoon cocoa onto the top of the cake. Cut in 3/4-inch slices.

Filling

1 In a medium bowl, cream butter until light.

2 Sift together the confectioner's sugar and cocoa and beat into butter. Add a few drops of milk to bring to spreading consistency.

Variation

• 1 cup of whipped cream may be used instead of buttercream. Refrigerate unused portions.

Irene Soos

White Cake Roll

Fehér tekercs

This sponge is customized to American preferences. The addition of a bit of oil makes the cake moist.

6 jumbo eggs, separated

1/8 teaspoon baking powder

1 tablespoon oil

5 tablespoons sugar

Buttercream Filling

3/4 pound (3 sticks) unsalted butter

1 cup confectioner's sugar

1/2 teaspoon vanilla

Line a 15 x 10 x 1-inch pan with aluminum foil, matte side up, with enough over the edge to lift the cake out when done. Preheat oven to 350°.

1 In a large bowl, beat egg whites until they form very stiff peaks.

2 Place egg yolks in another large bowl and add baking powder, oil and sugar. Mix well, until smooth.

3 Fold the yolk mixture into the egg whites with a spatula until well blended. Pour into the prepared pan and spread evenly.

4 Bake for about 15 minutes until a toothpick tester comes out clean. Lift the cake out of the pan with the edges of the foil. Invert it onto a clean dish towel; leave the foil in place. Let cool 15 minutes. Roll the cake jelly roll style with the foil and cool completely.

5 Unroll and remove foil. Spread with buttercream and roll up gently so as not to push the cream out the ends.

Variation

• For cocoa buttercream filling, see page 146.

Ethel Nagy

Coffee Torte

Kávé torta

Coffee flavored sponge cake is lavished with a rich, cooked coffee-cocoa frosting.

8 eggs, separated

2 cups sugar

2 cups flour

1 cup strong black coffee

1 teaspoon vanilla

4 teaspoons baking powder

Grease and flour two 9-inch baking pans. Preheat oven to 350°.

1 In a large bowl, mix egg yolks with sugar, flour, coffee, vanilla and baking powder. Combine thoroughly.

2 In a separate medium bowl, beat egg whites until stiff. Fold into egg yolk mixture.

3 Pour into pans and bake for 30 to 35 minutes. Cool and release from pans.

Filling and Frosting

1 cup heavy cream

4 egg yolks

4 tablespoons sugar

1 tablespoon flour

3/4 pound (3 sticks) unsalted butter

3 tablespoons confectioner's sugar

3 tablespoons strong black coffee

1 tablespoon cocoa

1 teaspoon vanilla

Filling and frosting:

1 In a heavy saucepan or top of a double boiler, combine heavy cream, egg yolks, sugar and flour. Cook, stirring, until thick custard forms, about 15 minutes. Remove from heat and cool completely.

2 In a small bowl, cream together unsalted butter, confectioner's sugar, coffee, cocoa and vanilla. Add to cooled egg mixture. Refrigerate if soft.

3 To assemble the cake, position the bottom layer on the cake dish so rounded side is on the bottom. If round is too high, slice off the bulge to even the layer. Frost the middle, add the top layer, frost top and sides.

In memory of Mary Juhasz

Coffee Sponge Cake

Kávés piskóta

Semi-sweet coffee sponge cake enhanced by earthy nut meats.

1 tablespoon instant coffee

1 cup boiling water

2 cups unbleached flour

3 teaspoons baking powder

1/2 teaspoon salt

6 eggs, separated

1/2 teaspoon cream of tartar

1/2 cup sugar

1 cup sugar

1 teaspoon vanilla

1 cup ground nuts, walnuts, almonds and/or pecans

Coffee Frosting

2 tablespoons butter, softened

2 cups confectioner's sugar

2 teaspoons instant coffee rolled fine between waxed paper

2 tablespoons plus 3 teaspoons milk, as needed

Preheat oven to 350°

1 In a cup, dissolve coffee in the boiling water. Set aside to cool.

2 In a medium bowl, sift flour, baking powder and salt.

3 In large bowl, beat egg whites with cream of tartar until soft mounds begin to form. Add the 1/2 cup sugar gradually and continue beating until stiff peaks form. Set aside.

4 In another large bowl, beat egg yolks and gradually add the 1 cup of sugar and vanilla. Add dry ingredients alternately with cooled coffee to egg yolk mixture. Fold in nuts. Fold egg yolk mixture a little at a time into the whites. Pour into 10-inch tube pan and bake for 60 to 70 minutes. Let rest a few minutes and invert pan to remove cake.

5 When cool, mix frosting, adding milk until spreading consistency.

Karen Teigiser, in memory of Irene Teigiser

149

Dobos Torte

Dobos torta

Invented by the Hungarian confectioner, József C. Dobos in 1884, this cake was introduced at the National General Exhibition of Budapest in 1885. It quickly became the favorite of Emperor Franz Joseph I and Empress Elizabeth of Austro-Hungary, then most of Europe. It was the first to use buttercream filling, replacing whipped cream or custard fillings, allowing it to be shipped throughout Europe. The recipe was a guarded secret until 1906 when it was presented to the Budapest Confectioners' and Gingerbread Makers' Chamber of Industry. It became very popular throughout Europe. Over a hundred variations exist, this is one of them.

9 eggs, separated

1-1/2 cups sugar

1-1/2 cups cake flour

1 teaspoon baking powder

1-1/2 teaspoons vanilla

1/8 teaspoon salt

Chocolate Cream Filling:

Two 4 ounce bars German sweet chocolate

1/2 cup water

3/4 cup sugar

3/8 pound (1-1/2 sticks) unsalted butter

6 egg yolks

Caramel glaze

3/4 cup sugar

....

Chocolate Buttercream Filling Variation

1/2 pound (2 sticks) unsalted butter

2 cups confectioner's sugar

6 squares (2 oz each) unsweetened chocolate

2 teaspoons vanilla

Grease and flour 9-inch cake pans or grease and line with parchment to fit the bottom of the pan. Wash pans between use and repeat preparation for each layer. This recipe makes 7 to 11 layers. Preheat oven to 375°

1 In a large bowl, beat egg yolks. Gradually beat in sugar; mixture should be light. Add vanilla.

2 Sift cake flour and baking powder together. Stir into egg yolk mixture.

3 In a large bowl, beat the egg whites until stiff. Gently fold the egg whites into the batter.

4 Spread some of the batter thinly in the cake pans. You will need to make 7 to 11 layers, total.

5 Bake layers for 5 to 10 minutes. Set aside the nicest looking layer on waxed paper to glaze for the top of the torte.

Filling

1 In a small saucepan over very low heat, melt the chocolate and water. Cook very slowly until thick, about 15 minutes.

2 Add sugar and cook two minutes. Stir in butter and cook until all foam disappears; stir occasionally. *Continues next page>*

Dobos Torte

continued

3 In a separate bowl, beat the egg yolks until light and lemon-colored. Add chocolate mixture slowly to the eggs, mixing as they are added so as not to cook the yolks. Place bowl in a pan of ice water to cool. Remove bowl from the ice water and continue beating the filling until mixture is thin enough to spread.

4 Reserve some filling to frost the sides. Spread filling on each layer and stack layers.

Caramel Glaze

Oil or butter a sharp knife (for step 3)

1 In a heavy skillet over low heat, melt the sugar until it caramelizes, browns and is smooth. *Very hot! Do not touch!*

2 Pour caramel quickly over the saved layer on the waxed paper, spreading it evenly with a spatula.

3 *Work quickly* before the caramel hardens. Using the prepared knife, cut the caramel layer into 12 or 16 wedges. Let dry then immediately place the wedges on top of the cake

4 Using the reserved filling, frost the sides.

5 Fill a pastry bag with any remaining filling and pipe a design along the top edge of the torte.

Store unused torte in refrigerator.

Variation

- Press ground hazelnuts or walnuts onto the sides of the cake after frosting.

In memory of Mary Juhaz

151

Fluffy Sponge Cake

Porcukros piskóta

Lighter-than-air sponge, flavored with vanilla or lemon and almond extracts.

6 eggs, separated

1-1/2 cup sugar

6 tablespoons cold water

1 teaspoon vanilla -or- 1 teaspoon lemon zest

1/4 teaspoon almond extract

1-1/2 cups sifted cake flour

1 teaspoon baking powder

1/4 teaspoon salt

Fresh fruit or maraschino cherries

Preheat oven to 325°.

1 In a large bowl, beat egg yolks until very thick and lemon colored, about 5 minutes. Gradually beat in sugar. Beat in 3 tablespoons water, flavoring, then the flour, followed by the remaining 3 tablespoons water.

2 In a separate medium bowl, beat 6 egg whites until frothy. Add baking powder and salt and continue beating until whites hold a stiff peak. Gently fold into egg yolk mixture.

3 Pour into ungreased 10 x 4-inch tube pan. Bake on the lowest oven rack in a 325° oven for about an hour, until cake pulls slightly from sides of pan. Invert pan and let cake cool in pan before removing.

4 Serve garnished with whipped cream, fresh fruit or dotted with maraschino cherries.

Betty Hartman

Golden Coffee Cake

Aranygaluska

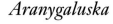

The consistency of this cake should be light as air so it pulls apart almost like cotton candy.

1 ounce
fresh cake yeast

1/4 teaspoon sugar

1 cup milk

4 cups flour

1/2 pound (2 sticks)
butter, melted

1 cup ground
walnuts mixed with
1/2 cup sugar

1 teaspoon salt

2 tablespoons sugar

4 eggs, beaten

Butter a deep-dish baking dish/pan

1 Gently warm the milk on low heat until lukewarm (100°-115° F.). Crumble yeast into milk with 1/4 teaspoon sugar and dissolve. Set in a warm place for 3 to 5 minutes until the mixture bubbles.

2 In a large bowl, mix flour with 1 tablespoon of the sugar and the salt. Add the eggs, 4 tablespoons of the melted butter and the milk-yeast mixture. Blend well. Cover with a clean towel and let rise in a warm place for 30 minutes or until doubled in size.

3 Scoop 1 tablespoon of dough from batter and place in bottom of baking dish. Repeat, placing each scoop next to the previous. Sprinkle each finished layer with sugared nuts.

4 Let rise in warm place until dough rises to top of the dish, about an hour.

Preheat oven to 350°

5 Bake about 1 hour, until golden.

Violet Sarosi

Hungarian Rococo Torte
Magyar Rokokó torta

The 18th century aristocratic Rococo style featured flamboyant, curvilinear forms in architecture. It was exemplified in Eszterháza palace. Qualities of elegance and luxury match this torte.

7 egg yolks

7 tablespoons sugar

7 teaspoons sweet chocolate

3 tablespoons dry bread crumbs

3 tablespoons flour

1 teaspoon baking powder

7 egg whites

Preheat oven to 350°.

Two 9-inch round cake pans, greased and sprinkled with few bread crumbs.(Reserve balance of crumbs)

1 In a large bowl, beat egg yolks with sugar until well blended.

2 Grate chocolate into eggs and sugar. Add bread crumbs, flour and baking powder.

3 In a medium bowl, beat egg whites until stiff. Fold into cake mixture.

4 Pour batter into prepared pans and bake 25 to 30 minutes. Remove from pans and cool.

Filling and Frosting

8 tablespoons sweet chocolate

2 tablespoons milk

8 tablespoons confectioner's sugar

3/8 pound (1-1/2 sticks) unsalted butter

2 teaspoons vanilla

Ground walnuts

Filling and Frosting

1 Melt sweet chocolate with milk in a medium saucepan over low heat. Cool.

2 Add confectioner's sugar and stir briskly until blended. Add unsalted butter and vanilla. Add enough ground walnuts to provide a heavy, but smooth texture.

3 Spread filling on top of bottom layer and position second layer over first. Frost sides and top of torte.

In memory of Mary Juhaz

154

Mocha-Chocolate Cake

Csokaládés-kávés sütemény

*This cocoa-coffee flavored cake is delicious plain,
frosted or layered with whipped cream and fresh berries.*

2 cups flour

3/4 cup
cocoa powder

2 cups sugar

2 teaspoons
baking soda

1 teaspoon
baking powder

1/2 teaspoon salt

2 eggs

1/2 cup vegetable oil

1 cup strong black
coffee, cooled to
room temperature

1 teaspoon vanilla

1 cup milk

Cocoa-Rum Frosting

1/2 pound (2 sticks)
unsalted butter

1/2 pound
confectioner's sugar

2-4 tablespoons
cocoa, as desired

1/2 teaspoon rum

*Grease and flour a 13 x 9-inch pan or two
9-inch round cake pans.
Preheat oven to 350°.*

1 In a large mixing bowl, place flour, cocoa,
sugar, baking soda, baking powder and salt. Add
eggs, oil, coffee, vanilla and milk and beat at
medium speed 1 to 2 minutes. Pour into pan.

2 Bake 35 minutes or until toothpick, inserted
comes out clean.

3 Cool 10 to 15 minutes and remove from pan.
Cake may be frosted as desired (chocolate,
coffee or cocoa-rum frosting), served layered
with whipped cream and fresh strawberries or
raspberries or dusted with confectioner's sugar.

Cocoa-Rum Frosting

Cream butter and mix in confectioner's sugar,
cocoa and rum. Spread over cake. Store any
unused portion in refrigerator.

Shirley Ferenczy

155

Moon Cakes

Kossuth-kifli

The Kossuth Craze described the popularity of Lajos Kossuth, Hungarian statesman and leader of the Hungarian Revolution. Towns, streets and apparently cakes were named after him.

3/4 cup (1-1/2 sticks) unsalted butter

1-1/2 cups sugar

6 eggs, separated

1-1/2 cups flour

1-1/2 teaspoons baking powder

1 teaspoon vanilla

Pinch of salt

1/2 cup ground walnuts mixed with 2 tablespoons sugar, to taste

Preheat oven to 350° Grease and flour a 15 x 12 x 2-inch pan.

1 In a medium bowl, sift flour, baking powder and salt and set aside.

2 In another medium bowl, cream butter and sugar until light and fluffy. Add egg yolks; beat until fluffy. Add vanilla and flour mixture.

3 In a large, clean, dry bowl, beat egg whites with pinch of salt until stiff. Fold into flour mixture.

4 Spread dough into pan. Sprinkle nuts on top. Bake about 25 minutes. Cut with 2-inch round cutter or top edge of drinking glass to form full or crescent moon shapes.

Variation

• Lemon juice can be substituted for vanilla.

Helen Marshalko; in memory of Rose Kaul

Nun's Cake

Apáca kalács

Surely nuns made more than one cake but this one may become a favorite baking habit.

1 ounce cake fresh yeast

1 teaspoon sugar

1 cup lukewarm milk

1 teaspoon salt

3 egg yolks

4 tablespoons lukewarm water

5 tablespoons sugar

1/2 pound margarine, melted and kept warm

4 cups flour

2 tablespoons cinnamon

1 cup sugar

1 In a small bowl, dissolve yeast in lukewarm water (100°-115° F.) with 1 teaspoon sugar. Set aside until it bubbles, about 3 to 5 minutes.

2 Add 5 tablespoons sugar, salt and warm margarine to the lukewarm milk. Add egg yolks and beat with a rotary beater.

3 In a large bowl, place flour. Make a well and pour in the milk and yeast mixtures, stirring with a wooden spoon until well mixed and dough forms a ball. Place in a bowl and chill overnight.

Preheat oven to 350° Grease 3 9-inch round pans

4 Divide dough in thirds and roll out each into a rectangle. Spread with nut filling or cinnamon sugar. Roll up tightly, jelly roll style. Place on pans and let rise, covered, until doubled in size.

5 Bake 45 minutes or until golden brown.

Violet Sarosi

Plum Cake

Szilvás sütemény

Studded with sweet purple plums, this cake is easy to assemble and is redolent of late summer's harvest.

1/2 cup oil

2 cups sugar

2 cups flour

4 cups purple plums, chopped

2 eggs

2 teaspoons cinnamon

2 teaspoons baking soda

1 teaspoon salt

1 teaspoon vanilla

1/2 cup chopped walnuts

Confectioner's sugar

Preheat oven to 350° Grease a 13 x 9-inch pan.

1 In large bowl, mix all ingredients well. Pour batter in prepared pan.

2 Bake for 40 to 45 minutes.

3 When cooled, sprinkle with confectioner's sugar.

Variation

• Instead of confectioner's sugar, mix 1 cup whipped cream with 1/4 teaspoon nutmeg and 1 tablespoon sugar. Serve each slice with a dollop of topping. Refrigerate any remaining topping.

Ethel Poulos

158

Poppy Seed Torte

Mákos torta

Buttermilk releases the nutty flavor of the poppy seeds, which pleasantly accompanies the citrus flavor.

1/3 cup poppy seed

1 cup buttermilk

1/2 pound (2 sticks) butter

1-1/2 cup sugar

4 eggs

2-1/2 cup sifted flour

2 teaspoons baking powder

1 teaspoon baking soda

1/2 teaspoon salt

1 teaspoon orange extract*

2 tablespoons sugar mixed with 1 teaspoon cinnamon

1 In a small bowl, combine poppy seed and buttermilk; refrigerate overnight to develop flavor.

Preheat oven to 350°. Grease and flour a 10-inch tube pan or Bundt pan.

2 In a medium bowl, sift together flour, baking powder, baking soda and salt and set aside.

3 In a large bowl, cream butter with sugar until light and fluffy. Add eggs, one at a time, beating after each addition. Add orange extract.

4 Alternately add flour and buttermilk mixture beginning and ending with dry ingredients.

5 Pour half the batter into the pan, sprinkle with cinnamon sugar and add remaining batter.

6 Bake for about 1 hour or until cake tester comes out clean. Cool 10 minutes, then remove from pan and finish cooling.

* *Variation*

• 2 teaspoons fresh orange or lemon zest may be used instead of orange extract for a light, fresh citrus flavor.

Ilona Grieve

Prune Cake

Aszalt szilvás sütemény

Prunes are underestimated in their ability to add depth of flavor and texture. This nutmeg-spiced cake is a classic.

1-1/2 cups sugar

3 eggs

1 cup oil

2 small jars baby prunes

2 cups flour

1/2 teaspoon salt

1 teaspoon baking soda

1 teaspoon cinnamon

1 teaspoon nutmeg

1/2 teaspoon allspice

1 cup chopped walnuts

1 cup raisins

Confectioner's sugar

Preheat oven to 300°.
Oil a 10-inch tube pan.

1 In a large bowl, mix together sugar and eggs. Add oil and then prunes.

2 Sift flour, salt, baking soda and spices into mixture. Add nuts and raisins and mix well.

3 Bake for 1 hour and 15 minutes.

4 When cooled, sprinkle with confectioner's sugar.

In memory of Rose Bodonyi

Sour Cream Coffee Cake

Tejfeles kávésütemény

Sour cream adds a lovely moist richness and smooth texture to the cake, contrasting the spiced, walnut layers.

3 cups flour

1-1/2 cup sugar

1-1/2 teaspoons baking powder

1-1/2 teaspoons baking soda

3/4 cup margarine or butter, softened

4 eggs

2 cups sour cream (1 pint)

1-1/2 teaspoon vanilla

Nut Mixture:

1/2 cup finely chopped nuts

1/2 cup brown sugar

1 tablespoon flour

1 teaspoon cinnamon

Preheat oven to 350°.

Grease and flour a 10-inch tube pan.

1 In a large bowl, mix dry ingredients together. Cut in softened margarine or butter as for pie crust.

2 In a small bowl, mix together eggs, sour cream and vanilla. Add to dry ingredients and blend thoroughly.

3 Pour one third of the batter into pan. Sprinkle with one third of the nut mixture. Repeat for two more layers.

4 Bake for about 1 hour until a cake tester comes out clean. Cool 10 minutes, then remove from pan and finish cooling.

Violet Szabo

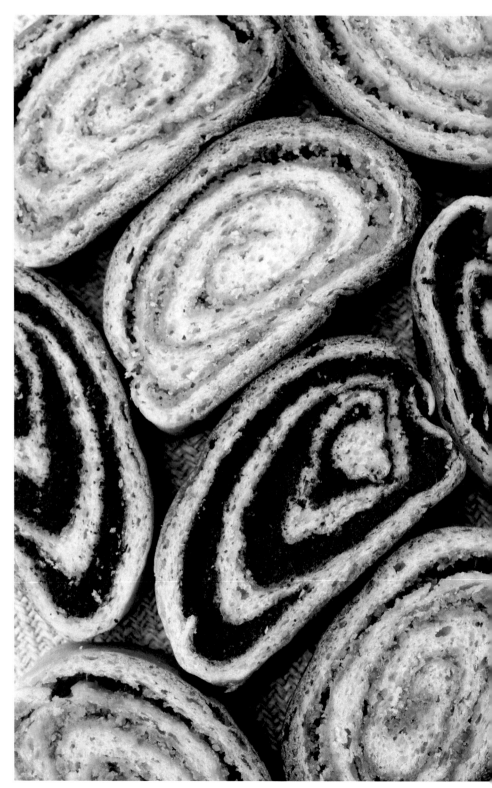

Nut and Poppy Seed Rolls – *Diós- vagy mákoskalács*, pages 178–180

PASTRY
& SWEETS

Doughnuts – *Fánk*, page 177

HUNGARIANS LOVE SWEETS AFTER LUNCH OR DINNER AND
AS SNACKS WITH COFFEE OR TEA. AMONG THE MOST POPULAR
PASTRIES ARE *PITE* OR *LEPÉNY* – SQUARES OF DOUGH TOPPED
WITH FRUIT OR CHEESE AND SOMETIMES FINISHED WITH
MERINGUE; *KALÁCS* – YEAST CAKE, PLAIN OR SPIRALED WITH
NUTS OR POPPY SEED; *KIFLI* – CRESCENT-SHAPED COOKIES
IN MANY VARIETIES; *FÁNK* – DOUGHNUTS; AND THE MOST
FAMOUS OF THEM ALL, *RÉTES* – STRUDEL. PASTRY MAKING IN
HUNGARY HAS LONG BEEN VIEWED AS AN EXACTING CRAFT,
REQUIRING TIME, EFFORT, SKILL AND PATIENCE TO CREATE
DOUGHS THAT ARE DELICATE, FLAKY, RICH AND LIGHT. SO
PRECISE WAS THE ART THAT OLD WORLD BAKERS' GUILDS
SPECIALIZED IN INDIVIDUAL TREATS, LIKE GINGERBREAD,
BISCUITS, CHOCOLATE, MARZIPAN, CAKES AND TORTES, OR
BURNT SUGAR AND CANDIES. WHILE THE VIENNESE PASTRY
CHEFS WERE RECOGNIZED AS THE REIGNING BAKERS OF
THE AUSTRO-HUNGARIAN EMPIRE, THE PASTRY CHEFS
OF BUDAPEST WERE THEIR KNOWN RIVAL.

Thumbprints	Jam Tarts	Nut Nests	Butter Balls
Pineapple Squares	Nut & Poppy Seed Rolls	Moon Cakes	Cherry Strudel
Apricot Squares	Cheese Squares	Austrian Butter Horns	Fruit and Nut Pinwheels
Gerbeaud Squares	*Kifli*	Apple Squares	*Palacsinta*

Lepény or Pite

Lepény – *a pie or tart, or pite, a pie cut in squares, are the household's "everyday" pastry – an equivalent of a bar cookie. Variations of short-doughs paired with fillings were dependent upon what was in the kitchen that day. Dough is layered with fruit, sweet cheese,nuts or a combination, and topped with a full or latticed crust or meringue.* Kocka – *more literally a square – refers specifically to yeast-raised puff pastry with similar fillings.*

Kifli

Kifli *defines the crescent-shape of the cookie or bread roll more so than the dough or fillings, which are quite varied. The crescent shape of both kifli and moon cakes are symbolic of a Hungarian defeat of Ottoman Turks. Legend recounts that the invasion of Buda in 1686 was tipped off by pre-dawn Hungarian bakers who, to commemorate their heroic efforts, later baked the bread in the crescent shape of the Turkish Empire's emblem.*[5]

Kalács

Any sweet yeast-raised cake, is kalács. *Nut or poppy seeds rolls may be* kalács *or others refer to them as* bejgli. *The cake may be plain or filled.*

Rétes

Rétes *is the Hungarian word for strudel. Derived from the Turkish baklava phyllo dough, strudel was a traditional pastry in the Austro-Hungarian empire. The high gluten, elastic dough is stretched to translucent thinness, requiring much practice (and a large table) to achieve. Thawed phyllo dough as a satisfactory shortcut for strudel-making at home, though it is somewhat thicker than hand drawn strudel dough. Apple, cheese and cherry are popular sweet fillings. Cabbage or squash/pumpkin are examples of savory fillings.*

5. The Urban Fakanál. Andrea Miklós.
The New Hungarian Voice/
www.newhungarianvoice.com

Butter Balls

Vaja Labdák

An easy-to-make addition to a cookie tray and a classically rich, melt-in-your-mouth butter cookie.

1/2 pound (2 sticks) unsalted butter

1/2 cup sugar

2 egg yolks

2-3/4 cups flour

Preheat oven to 325°.

1 In a medium bowl, cream butter, add sugar gradually, then add egg yolks. Beat thoroughly. Work in flour. Roll balls the size of a walnut.

2 Place balls an inch apart on cookie sheets and bake until a delicate golden color, about 25 minutes. When cool, sprinkle with confectioner's sugar.

In memory of Ethel Kovach

Chocolate Walnut Cookies

Diós teasütemény

Walnut clusters are kissed with chocolate.

1-1/2 squares unsweetened chocolate, melted

1/2 teaspoon salt

1/2 cup flour

1/2 cup sugar

1/2 teaspoon baking powder

1-1/2 teaspoon vanilla

1/2 cup butter (1 stick), softened

1 egg

2 cups walnuts, chopped

Preheat oven to 350°. Grease baking sheets.

1 Place all ingredients except walnuts into a large mixing bowl.

2 Beat at medium speed until well mixed.

3 Stir walnuts into batter with a spatula.

4 Drop by rounded teaspoons onto baking sheets, 1/2-inch apart. Bake 10 minutes.

5 Remove to cooling racks. When cool, dust with confectioner's sugar.

Yield: 3 dozen.

Julianna Kovach Zingale, in memory of Esther Czinke

Date & Nut Bars

Diós-datolyás sütemény

Naturally sweet dates with added nutty crunch hook-up in this moist bar cookie.

3 eggs

1 cup sugar

1 cup flour

1/2 teaspoon baking powder

1 teaspoon vanilla

1-1/2 cup chopped dates

1 cup chopped nuts

Preheat oven to 350°. Grease a 13 x 9-inch pan

1 Beat eggs until thick and lemon-colored. Gradually add sugar and then vanilla.

2 Sift dry ingredients and gently fold into the egg mixture. Using a spatula, add nuts and dates.

3 Spread into pan and bake for 30 minutes. Cut into bars and sprinkle with confectioner's sugar.

In memory of Evelyn Komyati Unger

Walnut Thumbprint Cookies

Diós teasütemény

Nutty, fruity, rich and gone in a bite or two!

1/4 pound (1 stick) butter or 1/2 cup butter-flavored shortening

1/2 cup brown sugar

1 egg, separated

1 cup flour, sifted

1/4 teaspoon salt

1 cup of walnuts, finely chopped

1/2 teaspoon vanilla

Raspberry jam

Preheat oven to 375°.

1 In a large bowl, beat butter or shortening, brown sugar, egg yolk and vanilla. Sift flour with salt and blend thoroughly into the butter mixture.

2 Roll the dough into one-inch balls. Dip balls into slightly beaten egg white; roll in nuts. Place one-inch apart on an ungreased baking sheet. Bake for 5 minutes. Remove from oven.

3 Gently press thumb on top of the center of each cookie. Bake 5 to 8 minutes more. Cool.

4 Place about 1/8 teaspoon of raspberry jam into the thumbprint.

Yield: 3 dozen.

Violet Szabo

Cigar Cookies

Szivar sütemény

These are somewhat involved, but are a true testimony to Hungarian pastry making and worth the time and effort.

1 pound (4 sticks) unsalted butter, only

3-1/2 cups plus 2 tablespoons flour

12 eggs, separated, cover and refrigerate egg whites for use in filling the next day

Filling

12 egg whites

2 pounds walnuts, finely ground

2 cups sugar

1 Beat egg yolks in a small bowl.

2 In a large bowl, cut butter into flour as for pie crust. Using fork, add egg yolks and form into a ball. Cut into several pieces of dough.

3 On a pastry board, hand roll dough into long ropes, 1-inch diameter and cut into 1-inch pieces. Roll each piece in between hands to form balls.

Stack in covered container between sheets of waxed paper and refrigerate overnight.

The next day:
Preheat oven to 375°

1 Beat egg whites until frothy. Gradually add sugar beating until stiff peaks form. Gently fold in nuts.

2 Roll out each ball *very* thin and spread with 1/2 to 1 teaspoon filling and roll up like a cigar. Place seam side down on cookie sheet

3 Bake 10 minutes. Remove and while hot, roll each cigar in granulated sugar. Cool completely and store in a covered container.

These cookies are fragile so handle with care.

Marge Jacob

Jam Tarts

Lekváros aprósütemény

The dough contains no sugar so it lends itself to a variety of sweet fillings.

3 cups flour

2 teaspoons baking powder

1 teaspoon salt

1/2 pound (2 sticks) butter, cold

2 eggs

1/3 cup milk

Thick fruit preserves such as strawberry, pineapple, apricot, peach or nut filling

1 egg, beaten with a little milk

Preheat oven to 375°.

1 In a medium bowl, sift flour, baking powder and salt. Cut butter into mixture as for pie dough.

2 In a separate small bowl, beat eggs with milk and, using a fork, add to other ingredients, mixing until dough forms into a ball.

3 On a floured board with waxed paper over top of dough, roll very thin and with a pastry wheel, cut into 2-inch squares. Place 1/2 teaspoon of filling on the center of each square. Fold opposite corners to center and press to seal.

4 Brush tops with egg-milk wash and bake about 12 minutes until golden. Cool and sprinkle with confectioner's sugar.

Makes about 5 dozen.

In memory of Ethel Kovach

Tassie Nut Nests

Diósfészek

Americans use pecans, but Hungarians prefer walnuts. The added benefit is that walnuts yield a creamier filling because of their high oil content.

1/4 pound (1 stick) margarine or butter

1 cup flour

4 ounces cream cheese

Filling

1 egg

3/4 cup brown sugar

1/8 teaspoon salt

1 tablespoon butter, melted

1 teaspoon vanilla

2/3 cups coarsely ground walnuts

1 In a medium bowl, mix the cream cheese and margarine or butter until soft and creamy.

2 Add flour gradually and mix well. Form into 24 balls. Dough may be refrigerated 4 hours or overnight.

3 Press each ball into miniature muffin pans so the dough comes up the sides to the top.

Preheat oven to 350°.

4 Make the filling, be careful not to overbeat: In a medium bowl, beat egg. Add brown sugar gradually, beating well after each addition.

4 Add butter, salt and vanilla. Add ground nuts. Spoon filling into dough.

5 Bake about 25 to 30 minutes, less if browning quickly. Let cool 20 to 25 minutes. Remove from pans.

Emma Pentek

Fruit & Nut Pinwheels

Gyümölcsös-diós sütemény

A beautiful, colorful little cookie that looks festive on any dessert tray.

2 cups unsifted flour

1 teaspoon baking powder

1/4 pound (1 stick) butter or margarine, softened

1 cup sugar

1 egg

1 teaspoon vanilla

1 to 1-1/4 cup seedless raspberry or thick apricot jam

1 cup finely chopped nuts

1 Sift flour and baking powder and set aside.

2 In a large bowl, beat butter, sugar and egg until fluffy. Stir in vanilla. Gradually add flour mixture, stirring until thoroughly combined.

3 Roll out dough between waxed paper into a 10 x 12-inch rectangle. Remove top piece of waxed paper and spread jam evenly over dough, leaving about two inches plain on one long end. Sprinkle with nuts. From the long, jam-edge side, roll up the dough evenly, removing the waxed paper backing as you roll. Wrap the roll in waxed paper and refrigerate overnight.

Preheat oven to 375°

4 Cut roll into 1/4-inch slices and place on cookie sheets 2 inches apart. Bake for 9 minutes, or until golden at edges.

Caroline Lanzara

Ribbon Cookies

Szalag sütemény

A showpiece cookie! Take care to spread the doughs evenly so the layers look nice.

1 cup shortening

1 cup sugar

1 whole egg, beaten

1 teaspoon vanilla

2-1/2 cup flour, sifted

1-1/2 teaspoon baking powder

1/2 teaspoon salt

1/2 cup candied cherries, chopped

1 ounce unsweetened baking chocolate, melted and cooled

1/2 cup chopped or ground nuts

1 In a large bowl, beat shortening. Gradually add sugar, then egg and vanilla.

2 Sift flour, baking powder and salt. Add to shortening mixture and mix thoroughly.

3 Divide dough into three equal parts. Add cherries to one part, nuts to one part and chocolate to one part.

4 Line a pan with waxed paper so that it overlaps the pan both length and width-wise. Place the cherry dough on the bottom of the pan and pat evenly. Next spread the chocolate dough evenly over the cherry dough. Finish by evenly spreading the nut dough over the chocolate dough. Cover the dough with the waxed paper and refrigerate overnight.

Preheat oven to 350°

5 With a sharp knife, cut the dough in half or thirds, lengthwise. Cut width-wise in 1/8-inch strips. Remove cookies from pan and place on ungreased cookie sheets.

6 Bake for 10 to 15 minutes. Remove from cookie sheets and cool on rack.

In memory of Evelyn Komyati Unger

Cherry Strudel

Meggyes rétes

Adapting the Turkish phyllo (filo) used in baklava, Hungarians customized fillings with more variety than any other cuisine. Stretching strudel dough to translucent thinness takes practice to achieve. Phyllo dough is a satisfactory shortcut.

1-1/4 cups sugar

1/2 cup light brown sugar, firmly packed

1-1/2 tablespoon cornstarch

4 cups pitted tart cherries

1/3 cup water

2 teaspoons grated lemon or orange zest

1/2 teaspoon vanilla or almond extract

1/4 teaspoon allspice

1/8 teaspoon cinnamon

8 sheets phyllo dough, thawed

3 tablespoons butter, melted

1 tablespoon confectioner's sugar

1 *Prepare filling:* In a medium saucepan, mix together sugars and cornstarch. Stir in cherries, water, zest and vanilla. Cook over medium heat until bubbling and thickened. Reduce heat to low and add allspice and cinnamon and continue cooking, stirring occasionally for 15 minutes more. Remove pan from heat and cool completely.

Preheat oven to 400°. Grease baking sheet.

2 Unfold phyllo dough, laying them flat. Stack four sheets on plastic wrap. Brush top sheet with 1 tablespoon melted butter. Keep remaining sheets covered with plastic wrap and a damp cloth to prevent them from drying out.

3 Spread half the cooled filling along a short side of the phyllo dough. Starting with the short side and using the plastic wrap to lift the dough, roll up, jelly roll style. Fold ends under. Place seam side down on the prepared baking sheet. Brush with 1/2 tablespoon butter. Repeat with rest of dough, butter and filling to make a second roll.

4 Bake until golden, about 15 to 20 minutes. Cool on wire rack for 15 minutes. Transfer to cutting board to cool completely.
Sprinkle with confectioner's sugar.
Best when fresh and warm and crispy.

Variations

• Recipes for other fillings begin on page 206.

Violet Sarosi/American Hungarian Foundation

173

Angel Wings

Csörögefánk

Delicate "angel wings" are light, airy and celestial.

3 cups flour

6 egg yolks, slightly beaten

1/2 teaspoon salt

1 teaspoon sugar

3 tablespoons whiskey, rum or white wine

Shortening for deep frying

1 Sift flour, sugar and salt. Stir egg yolks and the whiskey or rum into the dry ingredients. Knead well. Cover with cloth or inverted bowl and let stand 20 to 25 minutes.

2 Roll dough thin and cut with pastry wheel into 3-inch squares. Cut two slits in each diagonally. Twist by pulling corners through slits.

3 Heat the oil to 350°, almost to the smoking point and then lower slightly. Deep fry three pieces at a time so as not to overcrowd the pan and to keep an even oil temperature. Fry until golden yellow and crisp. Drain on brown paper. Repeat process, maintaining proper temperature of fat.

4 Cool and sprinkle with confectioner's sugar.

Variation

• For a richer dough, use 8 yolks.

In memories of Irene Schnierer and Rose Kaul

Angel Twists

Heröcze

Angel Twists are a crispy, crunchy variation of Angel Wings.

1-1/2 cups flour

2 egg yolks

3 tablespoons sour cream

3 tablespoons sugar

1/4 teaspoon salt

1 teaspoon sugar

2 to 3 ounces of beer, wine or whiskey, more if dough is dry

Shortening for deep frying

1 Sift flour into large bowl and make a well in center. Work in all ingredients. Turn onto floured board and knead 10 to 15 minutes. Stretch and roll thin. Cut into 2-inch squares with pastry cutter.

Heat the shortening very hot then reduce heat a bit.

2 Cut a short, diagonal slit in the center of the dough and pull opposite end through.

3 Drop into hot fat. Turn when one side is golden brown. Do not overcook. Shake off excess fat and drain well, then finish draining on paper towels.

4 When cool, sprinkle with confectioner's sugar.

Tip:

• This is much easier if one person is making the twists and another is frying them. You must work quickly so the dough doesn't dry out.

In memory of Julianna Roczei

Doughnuts; Large Quantity
Fánk (nagy adag)

This is the First Hungarian Church's heritage recipe. These "carnival" donuts are best served warmed, dusted with confectioner's sugar.

30 pounds flour, less 4 cups

3/4 cups salt

9 scant cups sugar

1 pound (4 sticks) butter

1 pound (4 sticks) margarine

2 gallons milk

1/2 pound yeast

1/2 cup lemon juice

3-1/2 dozen eggs, less 6 egg whites, beaten

About 10 lbs of fat, SuperFry and pure lard per pan

1 Mix flour and salt; warm milk to lukewarm. Melt butter and margarine and set aside.

2 Dissolve yeast in about 2 cups of the milk. Add a little sugar to the yeast. Let rise.

3 After milk is warm, add the rest of the sugar, stirring to dissolve. Add eggs. Add butter, yeast mixture and lemon juice to milk and egg mixture. Mix into flour and beat 10 minutes.

4 Place in greased pan; grease top of dough; cover with cloth and let rise 1 hour.

5 Take part of dough; place on well floured board; pat out to slightly less than 1/2-inch thickness. Cut with a round cutter (3-inch is our standard; they will double in size). Place on floured cloth and let rise 30 minutes.

6 Heat shortening to very hot. Make holes in dough by pushing thumb through the center of each just before placing in hot fat. Adjust amount of fat depending on size of pan. Brown one side and turn, brown the opposite side until nicely browned.

7 Remove, and drain on paper towels.

Makes 30-33 dozen

First Hungarian Reformed Church Doughnut Makers and in memory of Julia Szonyi

Raised Doughnuts; Small Quan

Fánk (kis adag)

This smaller recipe may better suit you kitchen.

1-1/2 pounds (6 sticks) unsalted butter, melted, cooled to 80 to 100°

3 cups milk, scald and cooled to 80-110°

4 tablespoons sugar

1 teaspoon kosher salt

3 teaspoons yeast

2 pounds flour

4 egg yolks, lightly beaten

1 tablespoon lemon zest

Canola oil or shortening for deep fryer

1 In a bowl of a mixer fitted with a dough hook, add sugar, salt, lemon zest, yeast and egg to warm milk and butter. Blend until a soft, sticky dough is formed.

2 Lightly flour a board. Turn dough out and knead until dough is smooth and slightly tacky, adding flour to board as needed.

3 Cover dough and let rise 1 to 1-1/2 hours.

4 Place on well floured board; pat out to 1/2-inch thick. Cut with round cutter. Place on a lightly floured pan, cover with parchment paper and let rise until doubled, about 30 minutes.

5 While dough is rising, heat oil or shortening to 375°. Make holes in dough by pushing thumb through the center of each just before placing in hot oil or shortening.

6 Begin frying with soft side down. Turn when browned and continue frying until other side is brown. Remove and drain on paper towels.

7 Dust with confectioner's sugar when warm and again when cooled.

Makes 4 dozen

Mark Shary

...ut or Poppy Seed Rolls #1

Diós- vagy mákoskalács

These yeast rolls are traditionally made during the Easter and Christmas holidays.

1 pound (4 sticks) butter

1/2 cup sugar

1/2 teaspoon salt

1-1/2 cups half-and-half or milk

6 cups unbleached flour

2 ounces of fresh yeast, dissolved in 1/2 cup warm water with pinch of sugar

6 egg yolks

Nut Filling

6 egg whites, stiffly beaten

4 to 5 cups ground walnuts

1-1/2 cups sugar

1 teaspoon vanilla

1/2 cup bread crumbs, if desired

Poppy Seed Filling

1 pound ground poppy seed

1-1/2 cup milk or evaporated milk

3/4 cup applesauce or mashed pears

1 teaspoon vanilla

Confectioner's sugar

1 In a large mixing bowl, sift four, sugar and salt; cut in butter. In a small bowl, beat egg yolks with half-and-half or milk.

2 Make a well in flour mixture and pour in egg-milk mixture and proofed yeast. Mix and knead. Let dough rest 10 minutes and repeat kneading and resting two more times. Add more flour if dough is too sticky. When dough pulls away from bowl, divide into 6 balls. Wrap each ball in plastic wrap or waxed paper and refrigerate overnight, or freeze for future use.

For Cheese Roll, recipe follows, use two balls.

Nut Filling: Using a hand mixer, blend the egg whites, sugar and vanilla. Add nuts and blend well. Add bread crumbs, if using.

Poppy Seed Filling: Blend all ingredients in heavy pan. Bring to a boil, stirring to avoid scorching and until slightly thickened. Cool.

3 Bring dough to room temperature.

Preheat oven to 350°.

4 Roll dough to 1/4-inch on floured cloth canvas or board. Spread filling and roll up, leaving an inch at the seam side. Place on ungreased cookie sheet, seam side down. Cover with a towel; let rise in a warm place 1 to 2 hours, until doubled.

5 Brush with beaten egg (for a shiny brown crust) or milk (for matte brown crust). Bake for 30 to 40 minutes. Cool briefly; remove from pan to racks to finish cooling.

6 Sprinkle with confectioner's sugar.

Sweet Cheese Roll

Turós tekercs

Lemon brightens the flavor of this cheese filling and the sour cream provides a velvety texture.

Two reserved dough balls from previous recipe

Cheese Filling

16 ounces cottage cheese, sieving optional

8-ounce package cream cheese

3/4 cup sugar, to taste

Grated zest of 1 lemon

4 tablespoons sifted flour

1/2 cup sour cream

2 egg yolks, beaten

Preheat oven to 350°.
Butter a 15 x 10 x 1-inch pan.

1 Remove dough from refrigerator and bring dough to room temperature, about an hour.

2 In a medium bowl, blend all filling ingredients.

3 Roll out one portion of dough on floured canvas cloth or board to fit the pan. Line pan with dough and spread with cheese filling. Roll other piece of dough to fit the top. Carefully place dough on top of cheese filling and pinch sides to seal. Pierce dough several times with fork.

4 Let rise, covered with towel for 1 to 1-1/2 hours. Brush top with beaten egg or milk. Bake for 35 to 45 minutes until golden brown. Cool in pan and sprinkle with confectioner's sugar before serving. Can be freshened in warm oven.

In memory of Evelyn Komyati Unger

Nut or Poppy Seed Rolls #2

Diós-vagy mákos bejgli

4 cups flour, sifted

3/4 teaspoon baking soda

1/2 teaspoon salt

1 package dry yeast

1/2 pound (2 sticks) butter or margarine

5 egg yolks

1/2 cup sour cream

Confectioner's sugar

Poppy Seed Filling

1 pound fresh ground poppy seed

1 cup sugar

1 cup milk

1 teaspoon vanilla

1 ripe banana, mashed

Nut Filling

1 pound walnuts or pecans, ground

1 cup sugar

5 egg whites, beaten to form light peaks

1 In a large bowl, combine flour, soda, salt and yeast. Cut butter into flour until it resembles coarse meal. Add egg yolks and sour cream to mixture. Blend well with hands. Cut dough into 4 equal parts. Wrap each in waxed paper and refrigerate overnight.

Preheat oven to 375°. Grease cookie sheets.

2 Sift confectioner's sugar on cloth or board. Divide each package of dough in half. Roll one piece of dough thin so dough measures about 15 x 12-inches. Spread with filling. Roll up from the short end. Repeat with remaining dough.

3 Place rolls, seam side down on cookie sheets and bake for 20 minutes or until golden brown. When rolls have cooled slightly, run a knife under each and remove from cookie sheet. When completely cooled, sprinkle with confectioner's sugar.

Makes 4 rolls.

Poppy Seed filling:

Mix ingredients together. Fills 8 rolls.

Nut Filling:

Beat egg whites gradually adding sugar until soft peaks form. Fold in nuts. Use immediately. Fills 8 rolls.

Marge Molnar, in memory of Julia Molnar

Sour Cream Crescents

Tejfölös kifli

This is a classic, yeast and sour cream dough that is simply delicious.

1-1/2 cup flour

2 egg yolks

3 tablespoons sour cream

3 tablespoons sugar

1/4 teaspoon salt

1 teaspoon sugar

2 to 3 ounces of beer, wine or whiskey, more if dough is dry (or cook is taking swigs)

Shortening for deep frying

1 In a medium bowl, combine butter, sugar and salt.

2 Heat sour cream until hot but not boiling. Stir into butter mixture, stirring until butter melts. Stir in 1 cup flour until well blended. Add yeast mixture and another cup of flour. Mix thoroughly. Beat in remaining flour and eggs until smooth dough forms. Wrap dough in waxed paper. Refrigerate overnight.

3 Divide dough into quarters and roll into circles 1/4-inch thick. Cut each circle into 12 wedges and roll up from wide end. Place on greased baking sheet, pointed side down.

4 Cover and let rise in warm place until doubled in size, about 1 hour. Preheat oven to 375°.

5 Bake for 15 minutes.

Ethel Kardar

Nut Crescents

Diós kifli

Rich and flavorful, this yeast dough relies on cream for its richness. The lemon zest is a traditional flavoring and keeps the flavor light.

3 cups sifted flour

3 egg yolks, beaten

1/2 pound (2 sticks) butter

1 ounce fresh yeast or 1 package dry yeast

1/2 cup warm cream

1/8 teaspoon vanilla

2 tablespoons sugar

Nut, *lekvar* or apricot filling

1 egg, beaten

Nut Filling

1 pound ground walnuts

6 tablespoons sugar

Grated zest of 1/2 lemon

1/2 cup hot milk

1 Dissolve yeast in warm cream with sugar and vanilla.

2 In a large bowl, blend flour and butter thoroughly. Add egg yolks and yeast mixture. Knead thoroughly on well-floured board. Refrigerate dough for two hours or until firm enough to roll.

Preheat oven to 350° and grease cookie sheets

3 Make the filling by mixing the walnuts, sugar and lemon zest and stirring in the hot milk.

4 Divide dough in three parts and roll each into a 12-inch circle. Cut into 12 wedges. Place a teaspoon of filling on the widest part of each wedge and roll up.

5 Place on greased baking sheet, seam side down. Let stand for 20 minutes and brush top with egg. Bake for 15 to 18 minutes or until light brown.

Makes 36

Rose Kardar

Small Nut Horns

Kicsi diós kifli

No yeast is required in this rich pastry. The nut filling is spiced with a touch of cinnamon.

1/2 pound (2 sticks) butter or margarine

2 cups flour

1 egg yolk

3/4 cup sour cream or 1/2 pint

Filling

1/2 cup chopped walnuts

1/2 cup sugar

1 teaspoon cinnamon

Confectioner's sugar

1 Cut butter or margarine into flour as for pie crust. Mix yolk and sour cream and add to flour, mixing until soft but stiff. Wrap in plastic wrap and refrigerate overnight.

Preheat oven to 350°.

2 Mix filling in a small bowl and set aside.

3 Divide dough into thirds and roll out each ball on a lightly floured board to a 9-inch circle or more so it is thin. Sprinkle filling over dough and lightly press into dough surface. Cut into 16 triangular wedges.

4 Roll up each triangle, beginning at the wide end. Place point side down on cookie sheet.

5 Bake for about 20 minutes until golden.

6 When serving, dust with confectioner's sugar.

Jerry Takacs; Caroline Lanzara

Austrian Butter Horns

Osztrák vajas kifli

A delightful sugary crust surrounds thin, light pastry that almost melts into the fruit filling with each bite.

1/2 pound (2 sticks) unsalted butter, cold

3 egg yolks

5 tablespoons milk

2 cups flour

Confectioner's sugar

Thick fruit preserves such as apricot, peach, pineapple

1 In a medium bowl, cut butter into chunks. In a separate cup, whisk together egg yolks and milk. Pour over butter. Sift flour into bowl. With clean hands, squish and mix thoroughly until a soft, sticky dough forms.

2 Divide dough into 4 equal pieces. For each piece, pinch off 11 to 12 pieces of dough and roll between hands to form balls. Place on a tray lined with waxed paper. Refrigerate overnight.

Preheat oven to 350°. Line cookie sheets with aluminum foil and turn edges up about 1/4-inch to prevent filling from running off the sheets.

3 Work quickly in small batches on a wood or marble pastry board. Mound about 1/3 cup confectioner's sugar on board. Use a child's rolling pin or dowel rod (6 x 1-inch) to roll each ball paper-thin, flipping dough so that it is generously covered with confectioner's sugar. Place 1/2 teaspoon of preserves on one end of dough and roll up. Place seam side down on the cookie sheet. Lightly press ends to seal. Continue with the rest of the dough, adding confectioner's sugar to the board as needed.

4 Bake until edges are a delicate golden color, about 17 to 22 minutes. Remove each pastry immediately from cookie sheet placing topside down on a sheet of aluminum foil. When cool, gently turn right side up and dust with confectioner's sugar.

Julianna Kovach Zingale

Flaky Horns

Hájas kifli

Similar to puff pastry in preparation, repeating the folding, rolling, chilling process yields the flaky layers.

4 cups flour

1 teaspoon salt

1/4 pound (1 stick) butter

1 cup cold water

4 egg yolks

2 tablespoons white vinegar

1 pound vegetable shortening

Filling: nut, apricot, poppy seed or *lekvar*

1 In a large bowl, combine flour and salt. Cut in butter as for pie dough. Mix in water, egg yolks and vinegar. Knead dough in bowl 20 minutes. Cover and let rest 1 hour. Roll out to a square and spread with one third of the shortening. Fold dough in half, turn 90° and fold in half again. Refrigerate 20 minutes.

2 Repeat rolling out and spreading dough with shortening two more times, each time chilling after each roll and fold. Wrap dough in waxed paper and chill overnight.

Preheat oven to 350°

3 Roll dough to 1/8-inch thick and cut in 2-1/2-inch squares. Place small amount of filling in center of each square. Fold opposite corners to center and press lightly to seal. Place on ungreased cookie sheet.

4 Bake for 30 minutes or until golden brown. Cool and sprinkle with confectioners sugar.

In memory of Julia Molnar

Butter Horns with Prune-Nut Filling

Diós-aszalt szilvás kifli

This rich yeast pastry with lemon essence supports the thick, gooey and nutty filling.

5 cups flour

3 tablespoons sugar

1 teaspoon salt

1/2 pound shortening, half butter and half margarine

1 ounce fresh yeast, crumbled

2 egg yolks

1 whole egg

Grated zest of 1 lemon

2 tablespoons lemon juice

1/4 cup sour cream

Filling

1 pound cooked and seeded prunes

1 cup finely chopped walnuts

3 tablespoons sugar

1/4 teaspoon salt

1 teaspoon grated lemon zest

1 teaspoon lemon juice

1 Sift flour, sugar and salt into mixing bowl. Blend in shortening and yeast. Make a well in center and pour in egg yolks, whole egg, lemon zest and juice and sour cream. Mix well. Turn onto lightly floured board. Knead gently. Shape into a ball. Cover and set aside for 1 hour.

2 Divide dough in quarters. Roll out first quarter very thin and cut in rounds with an extra large cookie cutter. Place a teaspoon of filling on each. Roll dough around filling. Shape into crescents on cookie sheet. Brush with slightly beaten egg white. Repeat with remaining dough.

3 Let stand 20 minutes.

Preheat oven to 400° during that time.

4 Bake for 12 to 15 minutes.

Filling

Chop prunes fine. Add rest of ingredients and mix well.

In memory of Mary Kovach

Apple Roll (Mock Strudel)

Hamis almás rétes

Apple-filled pastry takes on many forms. Rolled into the dough and baked, it mocks strudel.

2 cups flour

1/2 pound (2 sticks) butter or margarine

3 egg yolks

2 tablespoons vinegar

1/4 cup water

Confectioner's sugar

Filling

4 cups peeled, sliced apples

3 tablespoons bread or graham cracker crumbs

1/2 to 3/4 cups sugar mixed with 1/2 teaspoon cinnamon

Raisins, optional

Melted butter

1 Cut butter or margarine into flour as for pie dough. Mix together egg, vinegar and water. Add to flour mixture and blend thoroughly. Cut dough into four pieces. Chill overnight.

2 Roll dough fairly thin on floured board or between sheets of waxed paper. Spread apples over the dough. Sprinkle with crumbs, cinnamon-sugar, raisins, if using, and melted butter. Roll up jelly roll style and place on cookie sheet, seam side down. Repeat with remaining dough.

3 Bake at 350° for 45 minutes.

4 Cool and sprinkle with confectioner's sugar.

In memory of Rose Kaul

Apple Squares

Almás lepény

These slices or "squares" are a traditional pastry with a lattice crust and thick, fruity filling.

2 cups flour

2 egg yolks

1/2 cup sour cream

1-1/3 teaspoon baking powder

1/3 cup shortening

1/3 cup margarine

1/3 cup sugar

Juice of 1 lemon

Milk or evaporated milk to brush top of dough

Filling

1/4 cup bread crumbs

5 apples, peeled, cored and sliced or 2 cans of pie filling

1/2 teaspoon cinnamon

1/2 cup ground walnuts

1/4 cup sugar

1 In a large bowl, sift dry ingredients. Cut in shortening as for pie dough. In a separate, small bowl, mix sour cream and egg yolks and add and to flour mixture, mixing thoroughly.

2 In another small bowl, mix nuts, cinnamon and sugar, to taste. Set aside 1/2 cup of the mixture.

Preheat oven to 350°

3 Divide dough in two. Roll to fit 15 x 10 x 1-inch pan, pressing dough 1-inch up sides of pan.

4 Sprinkle bread crumbs over dough; then arrange apples or spread pie filling, and sprinkle with remaining nut mixture.

5 Roll other half of dough to 1/8-inch thickness; cut into 1/2-inch strips. Place lattice style over filling.

6 Brush dough with milk; sprinkle with reserved nut mixture. Bake until light brown, about 30 minutes or more. Cool and cut into squares.

In memory of Julia Szonyi

Apricot Nut Linzer Squares

Barackos-diós linzer

Vary the filling with raspberry preserves or the more traditional use of red currant jam.

3 cups flour

Pinch of salt

3 eggs, separated

1/2 cup margarine and
1/2 cup shortening

3 teaspoons baking powder

1 teaspoon baking soda

1/4 cup sugar

Zest of one lemon

1/2 teaspoon cinnamon

1 cup sour cream

15 ounces apricot lekvar

Nut Filling

1 pound walnuts, ground

1 cup sugar

1/4 cup milk, more if needed

1 tablespoon margarine

Preheat oven to 350°

1 Make the nut filling: In a small saucepan melt shortening, add nuts, sugar and milk and cook, stirring over medium low heat until slightly thickened, about 10 minutes. Set aside to cool.

2 In a large bowl, sift flour with dry ingredients; cut in shortening and margarine as for pie dough. Add egg yolks and mix; add cinnamon and sour cream and mix thoroughly.

3 Reserve 1/3 of the dough for lattice top, pat remaining dough in a 15 x 10 x 1-inch jelly roll pan, including the side of the pan. Spread with *lekvar* and spread nut mixture over the top of the fruit filling.

4 Roll out remaining dough and cut in 1-inch strips with a pastry cutter. Weave crisscross to form a lattice on top. Whisk egg whites until frothy. Brush lattice with egg whites.

5 Bake for 30 minutes or until golden brown. Cool and cut into squares.

Mark Shary

Apricot Squares with Meringue Topping

Habos-barackos sütemény

The sweet meringue compliments the less sweet apricot filling.

3 cups sifted flour

2/3 cups sugar

2-1/2 teaspoon baking powder

4 tablespoons (1/2 stick) butter

1/2 cup sour cream

3 eggs, separated

1/2 teaspoon vanilla

15 ounces apricot *lekvar*

6 tablespoons sugar

1/2 cup ground nuts, such as walnuts

Preheat oven to 350°

1 In a large bowl, mix flour, baking powder and sugar. Cut in butter as for pie dough. Add sour cream, egg yolks and vanilla. Mix thoroughly.

2 Pat dough into 15 x 10 x 1-inch pan. Spread apricot *lekvar* over dough. Sprinkle with half of the nuts.

3 Bake for 30 minutes.

4 In a clean, dry bowl*, beat egg whites until frothy and gradually add sugar, beating until stiff peaks form. Spread on top of baked cake and sprinkle with rest of nuts. Return to oven and bake until meringue becomes a delicate golden brown color. Cool and cut into squares.

* *Tips:*

Wipe bowl with vinegar or lemon juice and let dry. This removes all traces of fat that would make the meringue gummy or sticky. Make this on a sunny, dry day for the best meringue.

In memory of Irene Schnierer

Jam Squares

Lekváros lepény

This all-purpose dough works with a variety of fillings.

4 cups flour

1/2 pound (2 sticks) margarine or butter

3 eggs

1/4 cup sugar

2 teaspoons baking powder

1/2 cup sour cream

Grated zest of 1 lemon

1 teaspoon vanilla

1 cup or more fruit jam or preserves

3/4 cup chopped nuts (walnuts and/or pecans)

1 In a large bowl, cut margarine or butter into flour, as for pie dough. Make a well in center of flour and add eggs, sugar, baking powder, sour cream, lemon rind and vanilla, mix well. Turn dough onto lightly floured board and knead until a smooth ball forms.

2 Place in bowl, cover and refrigerate 4 hours or overnight.

Preheat oven to 400°

3 Divide dough in two; roll one half to fit a 15 x 10 x 1-inch jelly roll pan. Spread jam or preserves over surface of dough and sprinkle with nuts.

4 Roll out remaining dough and using pastry cutter, cut 1/2 inch strips. Weave, crisscross pieces over filling to form a lattice.

5 Bake for 25 minutes at 400°, then reduce heat to 350° for 20 minutes.

6 Cool; cut into squares. Dust with confectioner's sugar.

Bob Bosan, in memory of wife, Irene

Cheese Squares

Túrós Lepény

A raised dough has a lemon-kissed, rich cheese filling.

2/3 cup milk

1/8 teaspoon salt

1/4 cup sugar

4 cups flour

1/2 pound (2 sticks) margarine or butter

4 egg yolks, slightly beaten

1 cake yeast dissolved in 1/2 cup warm water with

1 teaspoon sugar

Filling

1 pint dry cottage cheese, put through sieve

8 ounce package cream cheese

2 eggs

2 egg yolks

1 cup sugar

Juice and zest of 1/2 lemon

Icing

1 cup confectioner's sugar

Water, as needed

1 teaspoon lemon zest, optional

1 Scald milk; add sugar and salt and let cool to room temperature.

2 Cut margarine or butter into flour as for pie dough. Add milk-sugar mixture, yeast and egg yolks and blend thoroughly to form a soft dough. Divide dough in half.

3 Roll out one portion of dough to fit a 15 x 10 x 1-inch jelly roll pan. Place dough in pan and spread with cheese filling.

4 Roll out remaining dough and cover filling. Seal and trim edges.

5 Pierce with fork or cut slits with a sharp knife into top layer of dough. Cover; let rise until doubled in bulk, about 1 hour.

Preheat oven to 350°

6 Bake for 35 to 40 minutes.

7 Cool and either dust with confectioner's sugar or drizzle with confectioner's sugar icing.

Icing

Mix confectioner's sugar, lemon zest and just enough water to make a thin icing. Drizzle over crust with fork or whisk.

In memory of Olga Kish

192

Sweet Cheese Squares
Édes Turós Kockák

This all-purpose dough will also suit a variety of fillings.

2 cups unsifted flour

1/4 teaspoon salt

1/2 pound (2 sticks) unsalted butter, chilled and cut into pieces

1/2 cup sour cream

1 egg yolk

Sweet Cheese Filling

8 ounces cream cheese

1 teaspoon grated lemon peel

1 egg

1 teaspoon vanilla

Confectioner's sugar

1 In a large bowl, combine flour and salt and add butter, cutting in with pastry blender until particles resemble the size of dried peas.

2 Combine sour cream and egg yolk, and add to flour mixture. Using hands, form pastry into ball. Divide in half. Shape each half into 8-inch round diameter. Cover with plastic and refrigerate at least 4 hours or overnight.

Preheat oven to 375°

3 In a small bowl, blend the filling ingredients until smooth.

4 Roll each ball to a little thinner than 1/8-inch thick. Cut into 3-inch squares.

5 Place 1 teaspoon filling onto each square. Lay across top of ungreased miniature muffin pans. Press opposite corners together in center. Chill 30 minutes.

6 Bake for 30 minutes until browned. Remove from pan.

7 Dust with confectioner's sugar when completely cool.

Ethel Kardar

Linzer Torte

Linzer torta

Linzer is the oldest cake known with a recipe dated from 1653 in an Austrian Abbey, this classic features latticework to show the filling. Hazelnuts and red currants are the traditional flavor combination.

4 cups flour

1 cup sugar

1 teaspoon baking powder

1 teaspoon baking soda

1 teaspoon salt

1/2 teaspoon nutmeg or cinnamon

1/2 cup shortening

6 egg yolks

1/2 pint sour cream

16 ounces of fruit preserves, such as currant or raspberry

2/3 cups ground hazelnuts

Preheat oven to 350°

Grease a 17 x 11 x 1-inch cookie sheet

1 Combine dry ingredients in a large bowl and cut shortening in as for pie dough.

2 In a small bowl, mix egg yolks and sour cream. Add to dry ingredients. Reserve 1/4 of the dough.

3 With buttered fingers, pat the main portion of dough into pan and up the sides. Spread with any fruit filling.

4 Add enough flour to remaining dough to make it easy to roll out. Cut lattice strips with a pastry cutter and arrange criss-cross over the fruit filling. Sprinkle chopped nuts over the top.

5 Bake for 35 minutes.

Violet Szabo; Filling in memory of Mary Szabo

Pineapple Squares

Ananász pite

Hungary meets Hawaii, adapting a cooked pineapple filling in a flaky crust.

4 cups flour

1 cup sugar

1 teaspoon baking soda

1 cup sugar

2 eggs

1/2 cup (1 stick) butter and 1/2 cup shortening

Less than 1 cup milk (see Step 3)

Filling

20-ounce can of crushed pineapple with juice

1 cup sugar

3 tablespoons cornstarch

Preheat oven to 350°

1 *Prepare the filling:* In a medium saucepan, bring pineapple and juice, sugar and cornstarch to a boil and cook until just thickened, about 15 minutes. Set aside and cool to room temperature.

2 Place dry ingredients a large bowl and cut in butter and shortening as for pie dough.

3 Break the eggs into a measuring cup and pour milk over the eggs so the volume measures 1 cup. Add vanilla and pour into dry ingredients. Mix to combine.

4 Divide dough in half. Roll each half between 2 sheets of waxed paper to form a rectangle that fits a 15 x 10 x 1-inch jelly roll pan. Peel one sheet of waxed paper away from dough and position it over pan. Carefully remove the remaining sheet of waxed paper, so as not to tear the dough.

5 Spread dough with cooled filling. Roll remaining dough to fit over pan. Seal and crimp edges. Pierce holes all over top layer of dough with fork.

6 Bake 30 to 40 minutes until golden brown.

Mark Shary

195

Lattice Gates

Rácsos sütemény

A Hungarian pastry classic.

1/2 pound (2 sticks) butter

3 cups flour

1/4 teaspoon baking soda

Grated zest of 1 lemon

1/2 cup sugar

3/4 teaspoon salt

2 egg yolks

1/2 cup sour cream

1 cup thick fruit preserves

Confectioner's sugar

Preheat oven to 350°

1 In a large bowl, cut butter into flour as for pie crust. Add sugar, baking soda, salt and lemon zest. Make well in the mixture and add egg yolks. Mix well and add sour cream until blended.

2 Roll out 2/3 of dough to about 11 x 16-inches and line a 15 x 10 x 1-inch pan, with dough up the sides of the pan. Spread preserves over dough.

3 Roll remaining dough and cut with pastry cutter into 1-1/2-inch strips. Weave in a crisscross pattern to lattice across top.

4 Bake 30 to 40 minutes at 350° until golden brown. Cut into squares while still warm. Sprinkle with confectioner's sugar.

Carol Horvath

196

Orlandi Squares

Orlandi lepény

This dough is very rich and topped with a light meringue.

1/4 pound (1 stick) unsalted butter

1 tablespoon lard or shortening

5 egg yolks

1/4 pound confectioner's sugar

2 cups unbleached flour

1/4 teaspoon baking soda

Grated zest of 1 lemon

Toppings

Peach or apricot preserves

5 egg whites

1 pound ground nuts (walnuts)

2-3/4 cups (3/4 pound) confectioner's sugar

Preheat oven to 350°

1 In a large bowl, mix together all dough ingredients until well blended and smooth. Spread dough in a 13 x 9-inch pan. Smooth a thin layer of peach or apricot filling over dough.

2 In a medium bowl, mix topping by beating egg whites; fold in ground nuts and confectioner's sugar. Mix well and spread over fruit filling.

3 Bake 30 minutes. Cool in pan and cut into small squares.

Emma Koch

Double Decker Pastry
Emeletes sütemény

A beautiful and luscious addition to a summer picnic, or anytime.

5 cups flour

1 cup sugar

4 teaspoons baking powder

2 teaspoons baking soda

1/4 teaspoon salt

1/2 pound (2 sticks) butter

4 egg yolks, slightly beaten

1/2 pint sour cream

4 teaspoons vanilla

Layer 1

2 cups ground walnuts

1/2 cup sugar

Layer 2

Apricot or peach preserves

Preheat oven to 350°

1 In a large bowl, mix dry ingredients. Cut in butter as for pie dough. In a separate small bowl, mix egg yolks sour cream and vanilla and add to the dry ingredients. Mix well.

2 Divide dough into three parts. Roll out first piece on floured board 1/8-inch thick. Line in ungreased 15 x 10 x 1-inch pan with dough. Sprinkle with nuts and sugar.

3 Roll out second piece of dough and place over nuts. Spread dough with preserves.

4 Roll out third piece of dough; cut into 1-inch strips and cross, lattice style over top.

5 Bake for 25 minutes or until golden brown. Cut into diamonds or squares.

Dust with confectioner's sugar when cool.

Variations

• Use unsalted butter and add 2 tablespoons solid shortening for a flakier dough.

• Before baking, sprinkle the top of the lattice with coarse sugar for extra sparkle. Omit the final dusting of confectioner's sugar.

Marge Molnar, In memory of Julia Molnar

Latticed Chocolate Pite

Rácsos csokoládés pite

Chocolate and almond combination are Viennese-influenced baking traditions.

1-1/2 pound plus
4 tablespoons butter
(6-1/2 sticks)

5 cups flour

1-1/2 cup
confectioners sugar

Pinch of salt

1 lemon, zest grated
and juiced

4 eggs, separated

1-1/4 cups sugar

1/2 pound blanched
almonds, ground

1/4 pound
bittersweet
chocolate, grated
(4 squares)

1/4 vanilla bean, split,
seeds removed, skin
discarded

1/4 cup apricot jam or
preserves

1 egg yolk

1 teaspoon water

Preheat oven to 350°

1   In a large bowl, cut butter into flour to form
    small crumbs. Mix in confectioner's sugar, salt,
    lemon zest, juice and 4 egg yolks. Reserve 1/3
    of the dough and pat the remaining into the
    bottom and sides of 15 x 10 x 1-inch jelly roll pan.

2   Bake in preheated oven for 10 minutes. Remove.
    Set aside to cool; leave oven on.

3   Make filling: In a medium bowl, beat egg
    whites to a froth and then gradually add sugar,
    beating to form soft peaks. Gently fold in
    almonds, grated chocolate and vanilla bean.

4   Spread jam or preserves on cooled, partially
    baked dough. Spread filling over fruit. Roll out
    remaining dough to 1/8-inch thick. Cut into
    3/4-inch strips and form crisscross, diamond
    shaped lattice work over the filling. In a cup,
    whisk egg yolk with 1 teaspoon water and
    lightly brush over lattice.

5   Bake 30 to 35 minutes. Cool and cut into
    diamonds or squares.

Margaret Dono Robertson

Gerbeaud Squares

Zserbo szelet

This pastry looks as wonderful as it tastes. Its name-sake is the famous cafe-confectionery in Budapest; among the largest and most lavish in Europe.

3-1/2 cups flour

1/8 teaspoon salt

3 egg yolks

3 tablespoons confectioner's sugar

2 ounces of yeast dissolved in 6 tablespoons + 2-1/4 teaspoons warm milk (100°-115° F.)

Filling

3 egg whites

2/3 cup sugar

1 cup ground walnuts

1 cup apricot jam, divided

Chocolate Glaze

3.5 ounces dark chocolate (65%)

1/3 cup sugar

6 tablespoons water

3-1/2 tablespoons butter

Line the bottom of a 10 x 15 x 1-inch jelly roll pan with parchment.

1 In a large bowl, mix the flour, salt, egg yolks, confectioner's sugar and yeast mixture; knead thoroughly. Divide dough into three portions and roll each out to fit the pan. Line the pan with one layer of the dough.

2 In a large bowl, beat the egg whites until frothy. Mix in walnuts, sugar and jam. Gently spread half of the mixture over the dough.

3 Place the second layer of dough on top of the first. Spread the rest of the jam-nut mixture over the second layer. Cover with the third layer of dough. Prick dough all over with a fork.

4 Let stand at room temperature for 30 minutes. *Preheat oven to 350°*

5 Bake for 40 minutes. Cool until slightly warm. Run a knife along the edges to loosen. Place a cookie sheet over the pan and invert the cake so the bottom is the top. Remove parchment.

6 In a small heavy saucepan, combine the chocolate, sugar and water over medium low heat; stir until mixture boils. Cook and stir until the mixture thickens, about 3 to 5 minutes. Remove from heat, stir in butter until it melts. Cool slightly, so the glaze thickens a bit.

7 Pour the glaze on top of cake, smooth once with a knife or spatula. Set until firm. Cut into neat squares with a wet knife.

Ilona Csiba

Linzer Dough

Linzer tészta

This versatile dough can be used in several recipes.

1 cup sugar

3 cups flour

1 teaspoon baking powder

1/2 pound (2 sticks) unsalted butter, room temperature

Juice and grated zest of 1 lemon

3 eggs

See variations for additional ingredients

....

Streusel Topping

2/3 cup sugar

2/3 cup flour

4 tablespoons (1/2 stick) unsalted butter

1/2 teaspoon cinnamon, optional

....

Filling for Cheese Squares

1 pound dry cottage cheese

1 to 2 tablespoons sour cream

1 teaspoon grated lemon zest

Preheat oven to 350°

Grease a 17 x 11 x 1-inch cookie sheet

1 Combine dry ingredients in a large bowl. Rub the butter into the flour mixture with hands.

2 Add eggs and lemon juice and mix. If the dough does not hold together, add a small amount of milk or sour cream. If the dough is too sticky to roll with a rolling pin, work in a bit more flour.

For sugar cookies: Roll dough and cut shapes with a cookie cutter. Brush with milk or a beaten egg and sprinkle with sugar. Bake until golden brown, approximately 30 to 35 minutes.

For layer cookies: Cut identical cookie shapes. In half of them, cut a hole in the middle. Spread fruit preserves on dough without the hole. Lightly press the dough with the hole over the preserves and fill the hole with preserves. Brush top of cookie with egg wash; sprinkle with sugar and ground nuts. Bake until golden brown, approximately 30 to 35 minutes.

For filled bar cookies: Roll dough to fit a cookie sheet and spread with thick fruit preserves. Sprinkle with streusel. Bake until golden brown, approximately 30 to 35 minutes.

For cheese squares: Line dough in an edged pan. *For sweet:* add 1/2 teaspoon vanilla and sugar to taste to cheese filling. *For a savory:* add 3 large sprigs of fresh dill, chopped, to cheese filling. Spread over dough and bake about 35 minutes.

Elisabeth Biro

Layered Butter Pastry

Vajas sütemény

Unsalted butter yields a different flavor dough.

5 eggs, separated

1/2 pound (2 sticks) unsalted butter

5 cups flour, Sapphire brand preferred

1 cup sugar

4 teaspoons baking powder

2 teaspoons vanilla

Sour cream

1/2 cup ground walnuts mixed with sugar to taste

Apricot or pineapple filling

Preheat oven to 375°

1 In a small bowl, beat egg whites. Divide in half and use half in the dough, reserve balance for top of pastry.

2 In a large bowl work ingredients together to form a smooth, soft dough. Add just enough sour cream to hold dough together and make it easy to roll. Divide dough into three portions.

3 Roll one portion of dough to 1/2-inch thick and line an 18 x 12-inch cookie sheet. Sprinkle generously with the nut-sugar mixture.

4 Roll the second dough portion thin and cover the nut layer. Spread with apricot or pineapple filling.

5 Roll the third dough portion thin and cover the fruit filling. Spread the remaining egg whites on the dough and sprinkle lightly with the remaining ground nuts and sugar mixture.

6 Bake 45 minutes or until lightly browned. Cool in pan. Cut into squares.

In memory of Emma Ozsvath

Hungarian Filled Pancakes
Palacsinta

Served as dessert or for light meal, palacsinta *perfection is mastered by a rolling twist of the wrist to coat the bottom of the pan with batter.*

1 cup flour

2-1/2 tablespoons sugar

Pinch of salt

3 eggs, well beaten

1 cup milk

1/4 cup water or club soda

2 tablespoons sour cream

Filling Options
Fruit preserves, poppy seed, nuts or creamed or dry cottage cheese mixed with sugar, to taste, with or without preserves

1 In a bowl, whisk all ingredients, until smooth.

2 Melt 1/2 teaspoon butter or margarine in a 7 to 8-inch skillet or crepe pan. Pour a small amount of batter into the center of the pan and rotate so the batter evenly covers the pan.

3 Cook over low to medium heat about a minute, until pancake is set and color on underside is lacy brown. Turn with spatula and heat other side, about one minute. Remove from pan to a plate.

4 Spread one end with filling, roll and serve, or keep warm in low oven until ready to serve.

May be sprinkled with confectioner's sugar and served either warm or cold.

Steve Sekeres, in memory of Mary Sekeres

Creamy Rice Pudding

Rizsfelfújt

The finishing addition of whipped egg whites lightens this pudding.

1/3 cup rice

1/4 teaspoon salt

1/4 cup
boiling water

2 cups milk

1/4 cup raisins

2 eggs, separated,
whites reserved or
pasteurized egg
whites

1/4 teaspoon salt

1 tablespoon
confectioner's sugar

1/8 teaspoon
cinnamon

1/4 cup sugar

1 In a 4-quart heavy saucepan with a tight fitting lid, boil water, add 1/4 teaspoon salt and rice. Cover, reduce heat to low and cook 25 minutes. If any water remains, drain.

2 In double boiler, heat 1-3/4 cups milk; add raisins. Cook about 15 minutes. Stir in cooked rice and cook 5 minutes more.

3 In a small bowl, combine slightly beaten egg yolks, with remaining 1/4 cup milk. Stir into hot rice with 1/4 teaspoon salt, confectioner's sugar and cinnamon. Cook 2 to 3 minutes; stir. Remove from heat.

4 While cooling, beat egg whites until frothy and gradually add sugar to form soft peaks. Fold sweetened egg whites into rice.

May be served with browned butter poured on top just before serving.

Serves 6

Baked Rice & Raisins Squares

Rizsfelfújt mazsolával/Rizs kuglóf

The gentle cooking process over the double boiler and length of cooking time results in an extra creamy pudding.

1 cup rice

1 quart milk

4 tablespoons (1/2 stick) butter or margarine

4 large egg yolks

Grated zest of a fresh lemon

1 cup sugar, more or less to taste

5 egg whites, stiffly beaten

1/2 cup raisins

1/4 cup bread crumbs

Preheat oven to 350°

1 Rinse rice and place in 4 quart saucepan. Add milk; bring to boil, stirring constantly to keep from sticking and scorching. Continue to stir and cook another 5 minutes. Stir in butter; remove from heat, cover and set aside for 15 minutes. *or until cooled*

2 In a medium bowl, beat egg yolks; add sugar and lemon zest. Add mixture to warm rice; blend gently. Fold into egg whites. Sprinkle a 8 x 8-inch glass baking dish with bread crumbs. Pour batter into dish. Bake for 45 to 50 minutes or until knife comes out clean when tested.

Cut into squares. *the best one*

Variation

• Substitute vanilla, orange zest or cinnamon for lemon zest.

In memory of Evelyn Komyati Unger

Fillings

Töltelékek

These are popular fillings for pastries.

Apricot Butter Filling

1 pound
dried apricots

1-1/2 cup water

1/2 cup of sugar

1 teaspoon grated
lemon or orange zest,
optional

1 In a medium saucepan, cook all ingredients over medium heat until apricots are soft and mixture thickens, about 30 minutes. Cool to room temperature.

2 Puree mixture in food processor. May be stored, covered, in refrigerator up to 2 weeks.

Apple Filling for Strudel

1/4 cup melted butter

1/2 cup toasted
fine bread crumbs

1/2 cup chopped
walnuts

3/4 cup sugar

2 pounds appled,
peeled

1/4 cup yellow raisins

1 Sprinkle dough with melted butter.

2 Mix walnuts and crumbs and sprinkle over buttered dough.

3 Slice or coarsely chop apples. Combine apples, raisins and sugar and put over crumbs. Roll strudel and cut to fit buttered pan.

4 Bake at 450° about 40 minutes until crisp and browned.

Cabbage Filling for Strudel

1 medium head
green cabbage

1/4 pound butter

1 teaspoon salt

3/4 teaspoon sugar

1 medium onion

1/4 teaspoon pepper

1 Grate cabbage.

2 In a large frying pan, melt butter and add cabbage, onion, salt, sugar and pepper. Cook over low heat, stirring, until cabbage is tender, about (20) minutes.

3 Cool before spreading on dough.

206

Fillings

Töltelékek

Cheese Filling for Strudel

1 pound pot cheese

2 egg yolks

2 egg whites,
whipped

1/2 cup sugar

1/2 teaspoon vanilla

4 tablespoons
sour cream

Mix ingredients and spread on dough.

Cottage Cheese and Raisin Filling

2 pounds
dry cottage cheese

1/4 pound (1 stick)
butter, softened

4 egg yolks; whites
reserved (see below)

4 tablespoons
sour cream

1 cup sugar

1 teaspoon salt

1 teaspoon vanilla

2 teaspoons grated
lemon zest

1/4 cup raisins

Reserved egg whites,
beaten to soft peaks

Mix ingredients in order given up to raisins.
Fold in egg whites. Use on dough for squares
and bake about 25 minutes.

Variation

• Golden (Sultana) raisins may be substituted
for brown raisins, which provide a more
pleasing color with the white filling.

More fillings >

Fillings

Töltelékek

Fruit and Nut Filling

1 pound cooked fruit	**1** Prunes, raisins, apricots, peaches, cherries or plums may be used for the cooked fruit. Chop fruit fine. Stew with a small amount of water until fruit is soft.
1 cup finely chopped walnuts	
3 tablespoons sugar, or to taste	**2** Add walnuts, sugar, salt, lemon zest and lemon juice. Mix well.
1/4 teaspoon salt	
1 teaspoon grated lemon zest	
1 teaspoon lemon juice	

Mushroom Filling for Strudel

1 small onion, minced	**1** In a small frying pan on low heat in 1 to 2 tablespoons of butter, cook and stir onion until translucent.
4 tablespoons (1/2 stick) butter	
1/2 pound button mushrooms, peeled and chopped	**2** Stir in mushrooms, salt and white pepper and continue cooking and stirring over low heat until the mushroom liquid evaporates. Cool.
3 eggs	**3** Separate eggs and lightly beat yolks. Stir into mushrooms. Beat egg whites until stiff and fold into mushroom mixture. Add crumbs.
4 tablespoons bread crumbs	
Salt and white pepper, to taste	**4** Spread onto strudel dough. Dot with remaining butter. Bake at 375° for 25 to 30 minutes.

Fillings

Töltelékek

Poppy Seed Filling

1/2 pound ground
poppy seeds

1/2 cup milk or water

3/4 cup of sugar

1 teaspoon
lemon juice and 1/2
teaspoon grated zest

1 tablespoon butter,
softened

1 Mix ingredients thoroughly and use immediately.

Prune Butter Filling

1 pound
pitted prunes

1/2 cup water

1/3 cup of sugar

1 teaspoon grated
lemon zest

1 In a medium saucepan, cook all ingredients over medium heat until prunes are soft and mixture thickens somewhat. Cool to room temperature.

2 Puree mixture in food processor. Use immediately or store in covered container in refrigerator up to 2 weeks.

Cooked Walnut Filling

2 cups walnuts,
ground three times

6-1/2 ounces
evaporated milk

1 cup of sugar

1 In a medium saucepan over medium low heat, stirring constantly, cook ingredients about 15 to 20 minutes until thickened.

2 Cool to room temperature before spreading on dough.

If God is for us,
    who can be against us?

Romans
8:31

Ha az Isten velünk,
    kicsoda ellenünk?

Rómaiakhoz
8:31

The First Hungarian Reformed Church at its East 79th location, Buckeye Road and in Walton Hills

Cleveland Hungarians
and the Reformed Christian Faith

The faith of the Hungarians has always been closely tied to nationality. In Hungary during the 19th and early 20th centuries, life centered around the church. It followed that Hungarian immigrants placed a high priority on worship and building churches, which were often the first buildings constructed in Hungarian-American communities. In 1891, the Reformed church – its doctrine based on the teachings of John Calvin – was the first to organize a Hungarian church in the United States, the First Hungarian Reformed Church of Cleveland, and the neighborhood emerged around the church. It was a vibrant life: the growing Cleveland Hungarian community, specifically the Buckeye Road area on the East Side, became well known worldwide. It is with God's mercy and grace that our faith and church have remained first in our lives and have been the unifying factor in our heritage and community.

The American-Hungarian Community and Buckeye Road

The Cleveland Hungarian immigrants and subsequent generations commanded a presence nationally for more than a half-century. Buckeye Road memories remain as a time capsule from that ethnic community.

The Hungarians' path to Cleveland began during the great immigration period of the late 1800s and continued through 1920. From the port of entry in New York, Hungarians sought Hungarian-speaking communities in New York City; New Brunswick and Passaic, New Jersey; Bridgeport and Fairfield, Connecticut; Pittsburgh; and Cleveland. Some moved further west into South Bend, Indiana and Chicago. Most immigrants were rural villagers and farmers who had hopes of making money and returning to Hungary to buy land. At first, many of the young men took jobs in coal mines, but the harsh, dangerous conditions led them to the steel mills and factories for work. The Hungarians possessed skills that prepared them to Americanize more easily than other Eastern European groups: they possessed a strong Christian work ethic, 89 percent[7] of the immigrants were literate, they were determined to earn higher wages, and they saved a large portion of their earnings.

Cleveland held the promise of industrialization, higher-paying jobs and a large Hungarian-speaking community. Families settled within walking distance of their factory jobs around East 79th and Woodland. Many initially lived in boarding houses run by immigrant women who washed and mended clothes, cleaned house and prepared meals; those run by Hungarian women came with the promise of good Hungarian home-cooked suppers. Aid was provided by the sick benefit societies which came into existence even before the church buildings and pastoral services. The societies provided money, food, care and assistance during illness, disability and unemployment, while offering the comfort of hymn singing and prayers and providing Christian burials. They brought faith, unity, support and security to the immigrants and increased in number as churches set up their own sick benefit societies.

Cleveland became an important center of Hungarian activity because of the dense Hungarian population, numerous Hungarian churches and local and national Hungarian organizations that flourished there. The First Hungarian Reformed Church of Cleveland (FHRC) was begun at the invitation of a German Reformed church in the East 79th Street neighborhood on Cleveland's East Side. (A Reformed church in

7. Thernstrom, Stephan (editor). *Harvard Encyclopedia of American Ethnic Groups* (Cambridge, Mass. and London: The Belknap Press of Harvard University Press 1980)

Pittsburgh followed shortly thereafter and then churches in South Norwalk, Connecticut; Trenton, New Jersey; New York City; and Mount Carmel, Pennsylvania.) Other Hungarian churches emerged in the Cleveland

Dedication of the First Hungarian Reformed Church, 1894

neighborhood: Roman and Greek Catholic in 1892, Baptist in 1903 and Lutheran in 1907, confirming the strong ethnic presence in the city. The Reformed churches comprised the majority of U.S. Hungarian churches by 1930, totaling 140 and outnumbering Hungarian Catholic churches by more than two to one.

The original First Hungarian Reformed Church was a wood-frame structure built in 1894. It was rebuilt in stone in 1904 and expanded twice. The buildings were the handwork of the immigrants, their hard labor testifying to their strong faith. The church was supported by the congregation (unlike the churches of Hungary, which were state-supported), and the members provided its upkeep. In turn, the church ministered to the congregation's spiritual needs – and its societal ones as well.

Over 43,000 Hungarian immigrants lived in Cleveland by 1920, representing almost 20 percent of the foreign-born population.[8] Afterwards, the Quota Acts limited immigration, and transient Hungarians who had previously returned to Hungary instead sought U.S. citizenship and permanent housing. Housing was less expensive on the outskirts of Cleveland, and this led the East Side Hungarian community to stretch its boundaries further east, moving "up the hill" – the full length of Buckeye Road as far as East 130th.

In 1925, the FHRC congregation purchased land at the intersections of Buckeye Road and East Boulevard to build Bethlen Hall, which was completed in 1932. Activities there and the minister's door-to-door collection campaign funded the construction of the church, which was finished in 1949 – in a mere eight months. Designed in the grand Romanesque cathedral style, the FHRC held an imposing physical position on "upper" Buckeye Road. Its soaring spire was visible for miles

8. Papp, Susan M. *Hungarian Americans and Their Communities of Cleveland* (Cleveland: Cleveland State University, 1981)

and a landmark to the Buckeye Road area. It
was later designated as such by the Cleveland
Landmarks Commission. FHRC's role was
pivotal in anchoring, developing and serving
the Buckeye Road community. The beautiful
church and large hall served as a religious,
cultural and civic center. It was instrumental
in providing Christian guidance and hope,
serving and caring for its community, aiding
immigrants and the poor and tending to
their needs. Social functions within the church provided entertainment.
The church also hosted visiting Hungarian dignitaries and Hungarian
Hollywood celebrities, among them Bill Dana, ZsaZsa and Eva Gabor,
Mitzi Gaynor, Ernie Kovacs, Tony Martin and Joe Pasternak.

FHRC kitchen workers at the 1949
dedication of the church building,
which was attended by 4,000.

Two additional waves of immigrants boosted the city's Hungarian
population. The post-World War II displaced persons (DPs, 1947-1953),
intent on preserving their heritage, maintaining their language and
reviving customs forbidden by the Communists, swelled the ranks of local
language schools and Hungarian scouting organizations. The Freedom
Fighters – escapees from the failed 1956 Revolution – also found their way
to Cleveland but were less inclined to hold on to their heritage. 250 refugees
were sponsored and settled by the FHRC congregation.

During the 1960s, the thriving Hungarian population in Cleveland
outnumbered that of every other city in the world except Budapest. Attended
by 1,200 families, with 3,474 communicants, the First Hungarian Reformed
Church constituted the largest congregation of Hungarian-Americans.

A Tightly-Knit Community

The Buckeye Road neighborhood remained tightly knit due to four factors:

1. The language and customs that marked their ethnic identity were
sustained by Saturday Hungarian school (which included religious
teachings and academic subjects), Hungarian summer school and Bible
school and social and civic organizations. Hungarian Boy Scout Troup 174,
begun in 1931, met for more than 30 years. Scouting activities for girls
and boys served the community and brought honor and recognition to the
FHRC. Daily Hungarian-language newspapers, the largest of which was
the *Szabadsag* (Liberty), served a community of more than 40,000 readers
in 1940 and was one of the city's last foreign-language papers.[9]

9. *Ibid.*

FHRC kitchen workers prepare dinners, fry fánk (doughnuts) and make noodles.

2. Surrounded by the foods, arts and language of the homeland, Hungarians in Cleveland found it easy to hold on to their traditional lifestyle. Specifically, Hungarian-owned butchers, bakers, stores, restaurants and taverns lined Buckeye Road, purveying Hungarian goods and good times. Delicious Hungarian food was served at church social events in large halls as well as in neighborhood eateries. Strolling violinists played Hungarian music in restaurants, keeping alive the tradition of serenading diners at Hungarian inns. Known for their skilled fencing techniques, Hungarians kept the sporting tradition alive by offering classes and demonstrations. Even theatrical productions became community events. Plays written in Hungarian and costumed, acted and produced by the neighborhood were well attended.

3. The churches, social and fraternal organizations played an important role in unifying the families and community, offering an abundance of activities: parades, card parties, dances, banquets, plays, lectures, and political meetings. Taking on an added roles of raising money for church

Hungarian parade along East Boulevard, 1952

operations and to promoting fellowship, congregations instituted picnics, bazaars and raffles. With seven Hungarian churches of all denominations within blocks of each other on the East Side (and four on the West Side), all supplemented by Hungarian organizations, the events were ongoing. Week-long summer Hungarian church camp united Hungarian youth from Indiana, Ohio, Pennsylvania and Connecticut. In addition to promoting religious renewal, ministers rolled up their sleeves and taught campers to make *palacsinta*, cook over an open fire in true Magyar style, sing Hungarian folk songs and learn to say table grace in Hungarian.

4. Neighbors shared a respectful familial-faith connection. Many of the families in the East Side community had been neighbors in Hungary; most members of the FHRC, from the Hungarian counties of Borsod, Abaúj-Torna, Zemplén, Szabolcs and Ung, traced their memories back to the same villages. They wanted their American lives to reflect their family heritage and their faith. Actions reflected respectfully back to family. Both allegiance to the Christian motto "cleanliness is indeed next to godliness"[10] and out of respect for what they had worked so hard to attain, Hungarian immigrants worked tirelessly to keep their homes neat and tidy. Neighborhood yards were lush with flowers, bushes, fruit trees, and vegetable gardens, reflecting a traditional love of planting, harvesting and natural beauty.

Yet despite these unifying factors, the American dream fueled the ambitions and hopes of the immigrants for their children's educational and professional success in America beyond Buckeye Road. Some parents insisted that their children speak only English. Slowly the Buckeye Road neighborhood began to disperse. Families moved first into nearby Shaker and Cleveland Heights to remain close to the home church, but later moved farther into the suburbs in pursuit of better jobs, schools and housing. Young adults took spouses from other nationalities. Some left Ohio entirely; California and Texas offered enclaves of Hungarian culture along with high-tech jobs and better weather, while Florida hosted retirees. The churches and Hungarian shops drew them back sporadically, but by the 1970s, the Buckeye Road neighborhood had changed. While a

10. Wesley, John. *On Dress; Sermon 88* (1769) Online reference: http://new.gbgm-umc.org/umhistory/wesley/sermons/88/

few of the older residents insisted on staying put, suburban sprawl had emphatically decentralized the Hungarian community. Most of the Hungarian churches moved into the suburbs, following their fleeing congregations. Homes started to deteriorate. As multicultured descendants were absorbed into American culture, churches merged and organizations disintegrated or dropped the "Hungarian" from their titles. As one of the last holdouts in the Buckeye Road community, the FHRC voted to build a new sanctuary, educational center and social hall in Walton Hills. Completed in 1995, it continues to hold worship in both English and Hungarian services.

Strong Spirit

The state of Ohio has long had a high population of Hungarian descendants who value their heritage. That legacy continues today.

Harvest festivals acknowledge God's bounty, giving thanks for the wheat and grapes that provide the bread and wine of Holy Communion. Celebratory events, especially the *Szüreti Bál* (grape harvest festival), feature Hungarian dinners, dancing and the performance of village dances by costumed children, accompanied by folk music played on authentic Hungarian instruments such as the *cimbalom*. Hungarian-Americans from Cleveland and their descendants countrywide return for these events to carry on the traditions and share memories.

The American picnic custom is enriched with the tastes of the Magyar *puszta*, including favorites like *szalonna sutés* (roasted bacon bread) and *laci pecsenye* (fried pork). All-you-can-eat stuffed cabbage dinners serve thousands of cabbage rolls to hundreds of hungry guests. Bake sales, featuring an array of luscious Hungarian pastries, are always highly anticipated events, with choices ranging from traditional everyday treats such as *kifli*, *pogácsa* (biscuits) and *palacsinta* (pancakes) to the more elaborate tortes, linzers and *zserbo* slices.

The Cleveland Hungarian Heritage Museum sponsors historical, political and arts events, speakers and exhibits.

The strong Hungarian spirit, with its faith, food, tradition and innovation, has enriched American life. *Élvez!* Enjoy!

Dancers at the Szüreti Bál, 2010.

217

Recipe Index

Anikó, Gergely. *Culinaria Hungary Culinaria*. Colonge: Könemann, 1999.

Bánfalvi, Carolyn. *Food Wine Budapest*. The Terroir Guides New York: The Little Bookroom, 2007.

Bennett, Paula Pogeny and Velma R. Clark. *The Art of Hungarian Cooking*. New York: Hippocrene Books, 2000.

Biro, Charlotte Slovak. *The Flavors of Hungary*. New York: Scribner, 1973.

Chamberlain, Lesley. *The Food and Cooking of Eastern Europe* London: Penguin Books, 1989.

Gundel, Károly. *Hungarian Cookery Book: 140 Hungarian Specialities*. Budapest: University Printing House, 1969.

Halász, Zoltán. *Hungarian Paprika Through the Ages*. Budapest: Corvina Press, 1963.

Hargittai, Magdolna. *Cooking the Hungarian Way*. Minneapolis: Lerner Publication Company, 2003.

Hemphill, Ian. *The Spice and Herb Bible: A Cook's Guide*. Toronto: Robert Rose, Inc., 2000.

Lang, George. *The Cuisine of Hungary*. New York: Bonanza Books, 1971.

Lang, George. *Nobodyu Knows the Truffles I've Seen*. New York: Alfred A. Knopf, 1998.

Levinson, David, and Melvin Ember. *American Immigrant Cultures Builders of a Nation*. New York: Macmillan Library Reference, 1997.

Luard, Elisabeth. *The Old World Kitchen: The Rich Tradition of European Peasant Cooking*. New York: Bantam Books, 1987.

Ortiz, Elizabeth Lambert. *The Encyclopedia of Herbs, Spices and Flavorings: A Cook's Compendium*. New York: DK (Dorling Kindersley, Inc.), 1994

Papp, Susan M. *Hungarian Americans and Their Communities of Cleveland*. Cleveland: Cleveland State University, 1981.

Sisa, Stephen. *The Spirit of Hungary: A Panorama of Hungarian History and Culture*. New Jersey: Vista Books, 1990.

Wechsberg, Joseph. *The Cooking of Vienna's Empire*. New York: Time Life Books, 1968.

Venesz, József. *Hungarian Cuisine: A Complete Cookery Book*. Budapest: Corvina, 1958.

Venesz, József. *Hungarian Cuisine*. Budapest: Corvina Press, 1958.

Venesz, József. *Hungarian Culinary Art*. Budapest: Corvina Press, 1958.

Zanger, Mark H. *The American Ethnic Cookbook for Students*. Phoenix: Oryx Press, 2001.

Zibart, Eve. *The Ethnic Food Lover's Companion: Understanding the Cuisines of the World*. Birmingham Alabama: Menasha Ridge Press, 2001.

This book was set in the typefaces Janson and Myriad Pro. Janson was selected as a tribute to **Miklós Kis,** the Hungarian who designed and cut the typeface in 1690.

A Hungarian theologian, Kis was sent to Amsterdam in 1684 by his bishop to learn the craft of printing and to print a Hungarian-language Bible. There he excelled in the art of engraving and punch-cutting letters for printing. Completing his studies in a single year, Kis returned to Kolozsvár, Hungary, where it was his dream to improve the cultural level of his people through literary exposure. He produced books in Hungarian and Latin on law, math, religion, and genealogy, along with tragicomedies and his autobiography, *Mentség*. In 1695 he printed the first Hungarian-language cookbook. Kis worked without sponsors, funding his projects through his own hard work and ingenuity. Kis designed and cut 17 new type fonts, complete with Hungarian accent marks, which were used for the text in all his works.